Curious Coffins

and

Riveting Rituals

Curious Coffins

and

Riveting Rituals

Death Practices Around the World

YY Liak

CHRONICLE BOOKS

SAN FRANCISCO

Library of Congress Cataloging-in-Publication Data

Names: Liak, YY, author, illustrator.
Title: Curious coffins and riveting rituals : death practices around the
    world / [written and illustrated by] YY Liak.
Other titles: Death practices around the world
Description: San Francisco : Chronicle Books, [2025] | Includes
    bibliographical references.
Identifiers: LCCN 2024061823 | ISBN 9781797230047 (hardcover)
Subjects: LCSH: Funeral rites and ceremonies--Cross-cultural studies. |
    Mourning customs--Cross-cultural studies. | Death--Religious aspects.
Classification: LCC GN486 .L53 2025 | DDC 393/.93--dc23/
eng/20250214
LC record available at https://lccn.loc.gov/2024061823

Manufactured in India.

Design by Wynne Au-Yeung and Barbara Bersche.

10 9 8 7 6 5 4 3 2

Chronicle books and gifts are available at special quantity discounts
to corporations, professional associations, literacy programs, and other
organizations. For details and discount information, please contact our
premiums department at corporategifts@chroniclebooks.com or at
1-800-759-0190.

Chronicle Books LLC
680 Second Street
San Francisco, California 94107
www.chroniclebooks.com

For Mom and Dad, who taught me how to live.

Death

Dead

Very Dead

HOW DO WE REMEMBER OUR DEAD? 117

Living

NOTES ON DYING 167

Death

A SHORT INTRODUCTION

"All earth was but one thought—and that was death."
—"DARKNESS," LORD BYRON

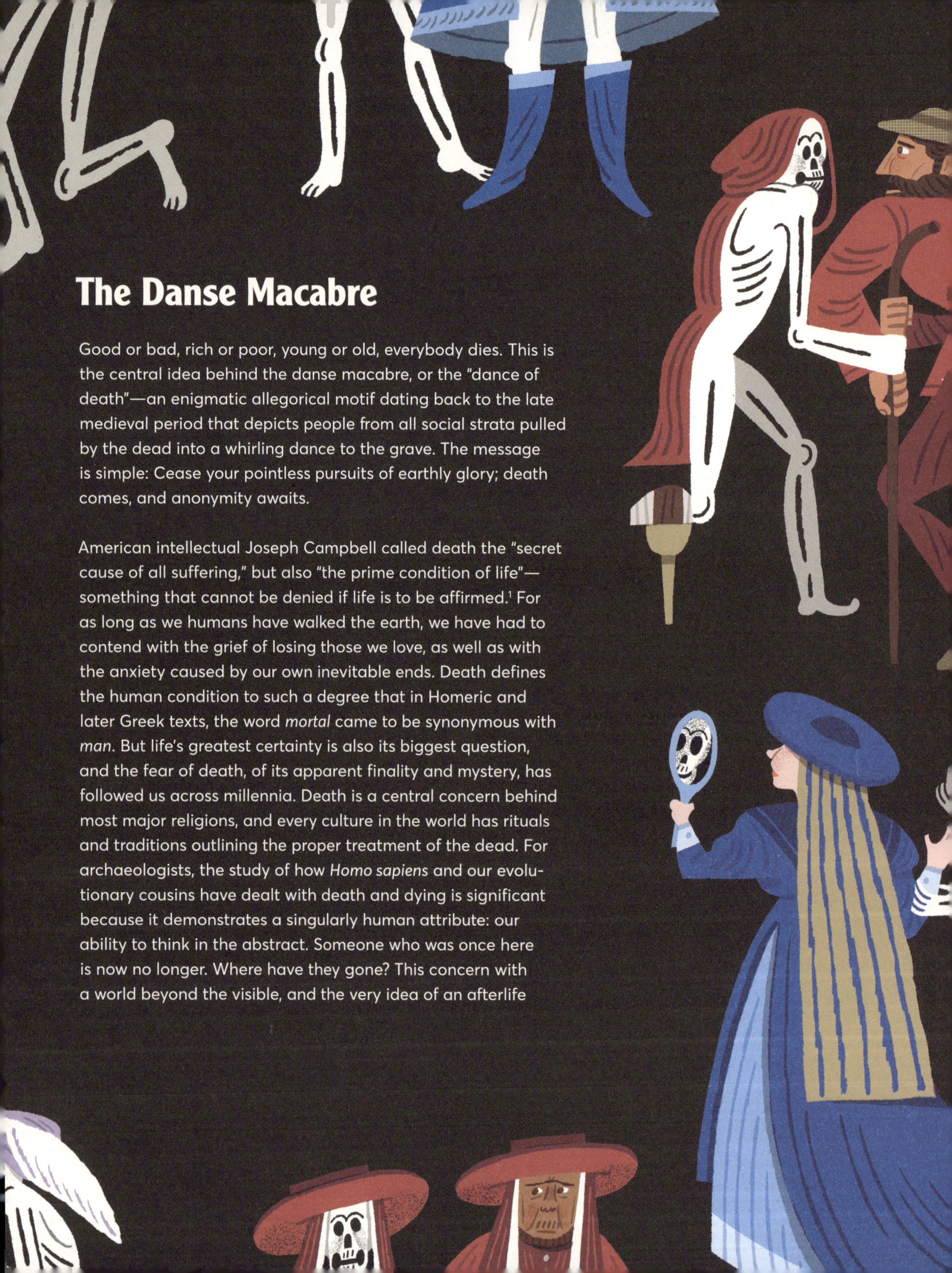

The Danse Macabre

Good or bad, rich or poor, young or old, everybody dies. This is
the central idea behind the danse macabre, or the "dance of
death"—an enigmatic allegorical motif dating back to the late
medieval period that depicts people from all social strata pulled
by the dead into a whirling dance to the grave. The message
is simple: Cease your pointless pursuits of earthly glory; death
comes, and anonymity awaits.

American intellectual Joseph Campbell called death the "secret
cause of all suffering," but also "the prime condition of life"—
something that cannot be denied if life is to be affirmed.[1] For
as long as we humans have walked the earth, we have had to
contend with the grief of losing those we love, as well as with
the anxiety caused by our own inevitable ends. Death defines
the human condition to such a degree that in Homeric and
later Greek texts, the word *mortal* came to be synonymous with
man. But life's greatest certainty is also its biggest question,
and the fear of death, of its apparent finality and mystery, has
followed us across millennia. Death is a central concern behind
most major religions, and every culture in the world has rituals
and traditions outlining the proper treatment of the dead. For
archaeologists, the study of how *Homo sapiens* and our evolutionary cousins have dealt with death and dying is significant
because it demonstrates a singularly human attribute: our
ability to think in the abstract. Someone who was once here
is now no longer. Where have they gone? This concern with
a world beyond the visible, and the very idea of an afterlife

we must prepare for, is something that, as far as we know, we share with no other animal. All living things are doomed to die, but *death*—or at least the symbolic and philosophical understanding of mortality—is ours alone.

But while we are all united by our mortality and its resultant psychological complications, our beliefs about death (and, by extension, the rituals shaped by those beliefs) can differ significantly from person to person. As we shall see, death may be understood as simply an end to life or as a transition to another state of existence. Some believe rebirth awaits us; others believe in divine judgment. Some think the dead go on to live in a world over, under, or separate from ours, while others think the boundary between the living and the dead is a porous one. All these ideas can hold significant sway over the way we conduct ourselves in life and the way we treat our dead. And for many of us, the "proper" way to deal with death is codified through death rituals specific to our communities.

A ritual may be defined as "religion in action,"[2] consisting of actions that tend to be "habitual, socially sanctioned, symbolic and without any practical consideration."[3] There is typically some degree of formality and conformity involved—knowledge of which is usually passed down from generation to generation. Rituals are baked into the very lifeblood of society. Whether you're a suburban American kid blowing out your birthday candles after making a wish or a Sateré-Mawé boy putting on a glove filled with angry bullet ants to mark your passage into manhood deep in the forests of the Amazon, rituals are used to mark moments of transition, such as birth, growing up, marriage, and, of course, death.

So why this ubiquity? Death rituals serve the same function as all others: They give us perspective. These ceremonies, which are often discernibly separate from the rhythms of daily life, help reestablish a common cultural understanding of how the world works and our place in it. Death, perhaps more than any other transitional event, represents a moment of extraordinary change. By giving us some much-needed structure during a time that can be incredibly disorientating, rituals help us make sense of the chaos. Customs and traditions also connect us with our community—not just with our immediate social circle but with the generations of people who have come before us, who have gone through the same grief and understood it as we do. In this way, rituals give us a shared purpose and identity, and regardless of whether custom calls for merriment or restraint, death throws into relief the most important cultural values by which people live their lives and evaluate their experiences. Just as death is a universal event, the desire to make sense of it through ritual action also seems to hold universal appeal.

In this book, you will be introduced to a number of death rituals across historical and geographical borders; perhaps some of them will be familiar to you, others not so much. It is impossible to overstate just how many different death rituals have existed throughout human history—certainly too many to jam into any one book. Nonetheless, I have tried my best to include those I consider significant (in that they fall under the world's major religions and are thus practiced by millions), moving, or just plain interesting. The death rituals in this book have been organized into several broad categories, despite the fact that many resist such casual classification. Some bodies are embalmed, then cremated; others are burned, then buried. A ritual's listing under one category certainly doesn't preclude it from fitting into another. It is also important to note that these rituals shouldn't be taken to represent entire cultures; in fact, you'd be hard-pressed to find any community that is entirely homogeneous in its beliefs and traditions. Rituals are fluid, and even those enshrined in religious dogma invariably pick up different local characteristics throughout time, depending on where they are practiced. The rites observed by a

Catholic family in Sicily might differ from those of a Catholic family in Mexico City; the former may adhere more closely to traditions codified by the Roman Catholic Church, while the latter might conduct ceremonies that draw from both Catholic and pre-Columbian Mesoamerican traditions (in a process known as syncretism). Some of the rituals discussed have since gone extinct, while others are slowly fading away. Some are observed by only a small but fervent minority group, while others are just now taking hold. All of this is to say: The book before you is in no way, shape, or form meant to be a comprehensive guide to mortuary customs, but I hope that it will serve as an enlightening introduction to some of the ways we humans choose to care for our dead. Because, of course, death rituals aren't actually for the dead; they're for the living.

A Brief History of Death

~90,000 BCE

The bodies of several pre-historic humans are buried, along with several stone tools covered in red ocher, in the Qafzeh Cave in the Jezreel Valley of Israel.

~40,000 BCE

A woman known as Mungo Lady is cremated and buried in the Australian outback's now-dry Lake Mungo, making her cremated remains some of the oldest we have on record.

~15,000 BCE

Multiple dead bodies are ritually consumed during the Upper Paleolithic Period in Gough's Cave, South West England, where archaeologists later find a cache of skulls that have been defleshed and fashioned into drinking cups.

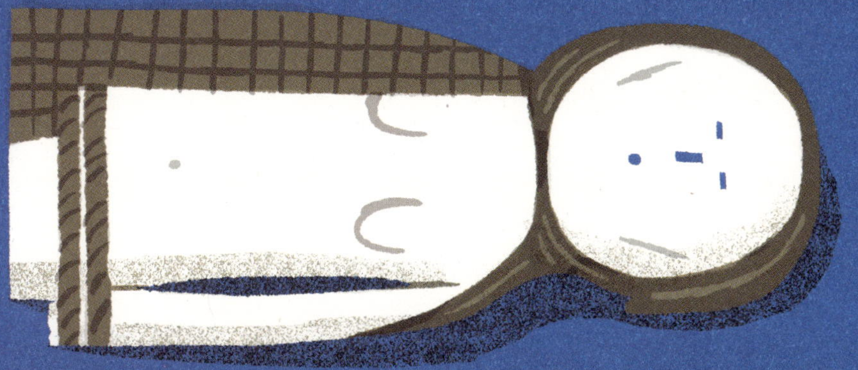

~5000 BCE

The Chinchorro of what is now South America mummify what become some of the oldest artificially mummified bodies we currently have on record before burying them in the scorching-hot deserts of present-day Chile.

~2600 BCE

The ancient Egyptians begin mummifying their dead, continually refining the technique over the next several thousand years until it slowly dies out between the fourth and seventh centuries CE.

246 BCE

Work begins on the massive subterranean tomb complex of Qin Shi Huang, the first emperor of China. Construction of the mausoleum (as well as the famous terra-cotta warriors that guard it) continues without pause until his death thirty-six years later.

Early Ninth Century CE

The first documented instances of Zoroastrians exposing the bodies of their dead on raised towers known as dakhmas are recorded by Persian historians in present-day Iran.

834 CE

Two Viking women are buried in one of the most famous and well-preserved ship graves in Oseberg, Norway.

1081–1903 CE

In the mountains of Japan, determined followers of Shugendō undergo a long and harrowing ritual of self-mummification known as sokushinbutsu.

1346–1353 CE

A bubonic plague pandemic known as the Black Death sweeps across Europe, claiming the lives of more than fifty million people—roughly 30 to 50 percent of the total European population at the time.[4]

1752 CE

The British Parliament passes the Murder Act, allowing for the dissection of convicted murderers. Eighty years later, the Anatomy Act is passed, allowing anatomists to work with donated cadavers.

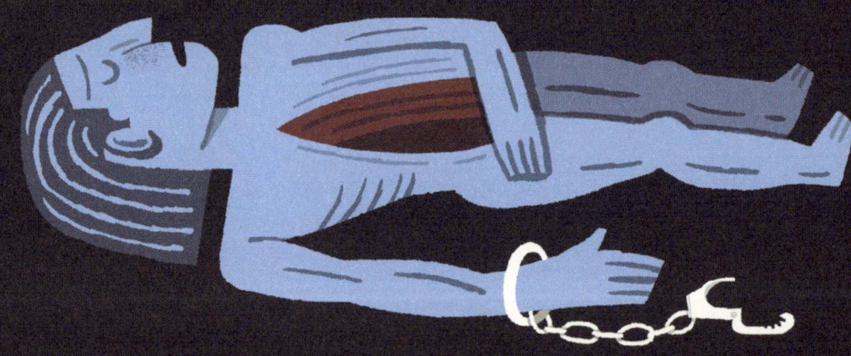

1849 CE

In Rochester, New York, the Fox sisters become the unwitting founders of a new religious movement known as Spiritualism. The movement, predicated on the belief that the living could communicate with the spirits of the dead, enjoys widespread popularity until its decline in the early 1900s.

1861–1865 CE

The American Civil War—the bloodiest conflict in US history—results in a death toll of more than six hundred thousand people, paving the way for the widespread popularization of modern embalming in the United States.

1914–1918 CE

World War I sees the rise of various military and techno-logical advancements that change the face of modern warfare forever, leading to more than forty million civilian and military casualties, includ-ing the six hundred thousand to 1.2 million people who perish in the Armenian genocide. Most die from malnutrition and disease.[5]

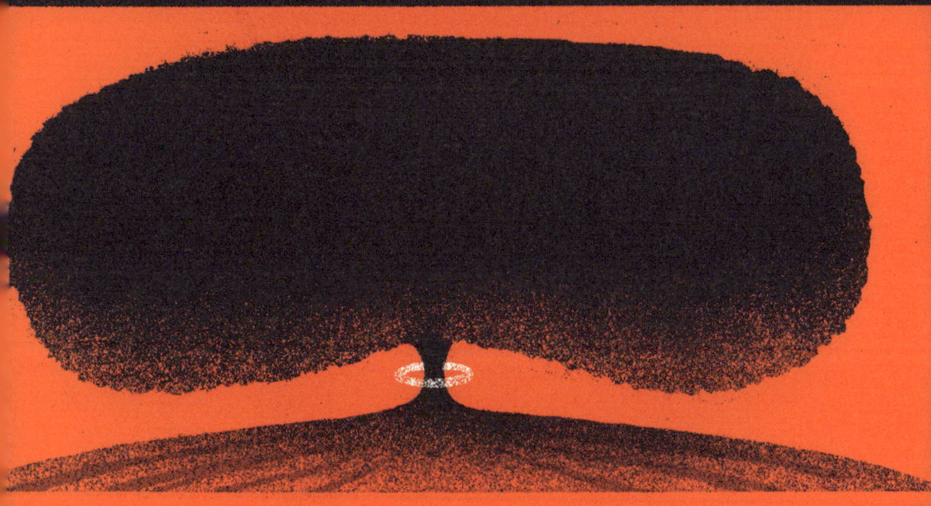

1939–1945 CE

World War II brings about the introduction of atomic weap-ons, and for the first time, humanity is confronted with the existential threat of total nuclear annihilation. The various theaters of war, disease, famine, and the Holocaust claim the lives of roughly seventy to eighty-five million people, making it by far the deadliest conflict in human history.

1990 CE

The Native American Graves Protection and Repatriation Act (NAGPRA) is passed, allowing tribes to begin reclaiming their cultural objects and remains from federal organizations and museum collections in the United States after more than four centuries of state-sanctioned pillaging, desecration, and theft.

Defining Death

What, exactly, does it mean to die? The answer might be more complicated than you think. In physiological terms, death is generally said to have occurred once a body no longer shows any observable signs of life. Up until very recently,[6] a person was considered dead upon the cessation of their heartbeat or respiratory system. However, advancements in technology and the introduction of modern methods of resuscitation meant that a heart could be mechanically restarted and kept alive, even if the patient never regained consciousness. Was that person alive, or dead? Suddenly, existing boundaries demarcating life and death got a hell of a lot hazier. In the United States, this change was formally enshrined in the Uniform Determination of Death Act, a law that allows medical professionals to declare a patient legally dead following the "irreversible cessation of all functions of the entire brain."[7] Adopted by most states in 1981, the law recognizes the brain as the seat of consciousness and the control center that maintains all basic bodily functions, making it the only organ that cannot be transplanted without significantly altering a person's identity. Today, brain death is identified through the presence of a persistent and irreversible coma, the permanent loss of one's ability to breathe, and the absence of all reflexes controlled by the brain stem. It is generally seen as the point of no return for patients, effectively allowing medical professionals to declare someone legally dead even if their body is kept alive on artificial life support.[8] Still, this remains contentious among medical professionals, and because some parts of the brain may continue to function after all the aforementioned boxes are ticked, there has been a push to revise the act. So the battle to reach a definitive consensus continues.[9]

But as we will see, the way we understand death goes far beyond a single biological event. There will come a time when our bodies fail us; physiologically speaking, dying is certain, even predictable, in how it unfolds across the board. And yet every death remains socially, metaphysically, and culturally distinct. While some view death as a complete and permanent disengagement, it is much more common, both globally and historically, for death to be seen as a kind of transition or transformation.[10] In fact, the idea of an afterlife is quite possibly one of the oldest concepts in recorded history.[11] Despite having not existed for billions of years before we were conceived, we seem to find it difficult to imagine ourselves returning to that state again.

All over the world, we see the same idea emerge: A person does not cease to exist the moment their heart and mind give out. Rather, it is believed that the self—that is, what makes you *you*—is beholden to neither mere flesh and blood nor the firing of synapses; it resides instead in something far more mysterious. Call it the soul, ātman, rūḥ, psyche, or what have you: This spiritual core is not so easily destroyed by something as mundane as one's earthly demise. Various systems of belief, including all the world's major religions, outline some form of an afterlife. Many seem to have reached astonishingly similar conclusions, sometimes completely independently of one another.

Where exactly each soul goes, however, is up for debate. Some religions, such as Confucianism and Shintoism, tend toward a more generalized domain of the dead, whereas others hold that our souls will be sorted into different otherworldly planes based on our various deeds and misdeeds. Although this belief is most commonly associated with Christian ideas of heaven and hell, the notion that separate kingdoms of pleasure and punishment await us appears throughout various mythologies and narrative traditions, from those of ancient Egypt to those of Chinese folk religion. In addition to seeing death as a transition, many also view it to be, like

Curious Coffins and Riveting Rituals

life, a transient state. Most followers of Buddhism, Sikhism, and Hinduism believe in reincarnation, which is the idea that one will be reborn into another physical form after dying in this life. All three of the major Abrahamic religions contend that everyone—alive or dead—will be brought forth to receive one final judgment during the end-times.

So if biological death doesn't signal the end . . . what does? For most of us, one's physical death is generally understood to be a conclusion, at least to this specific state of existence. But in India, a man on a pyre is only considered dead after his skull is broken and his spirit released.[12] On the other hand, in the remote regency of Tana Toraja, Indonesia, a person is only considered dead once an animal has been sacrificed and a funeral of appropriate opulence has been thrown in their honor; until then, they are simply referred to as being sick or asleep. In some South Pacific cultures, it is believed that little bits of life leave our bodies throughout our lifetimes, such as when we fall asleep or get sick, so it may be said that we "die" multiple times before finally passing on.[13] For communities such as these, death is not an event but a gradual social process.

How we understand the concept of death can affect the way we live long after someone dear to us has died. For some of us, the line between living and dead is clearly demarcated; for others, it is thin and porous. Some people venerate their saints in churches, others in their homes. Many believe that the dead can be powerful intercessors in their lives and those of their loved ones. Many communities have festivals that specifically revolve around communicating with and honoring their dead. Some believe that people's spirits live on, tied to objects or places of personal significance. Death might be universal, but the ways we define it sure aren't, and the more we learn about the different ways people approach death and dying, the closer we get to realizing that if we want to discover the meaning of life, we must first understand the meaning of death.

Death, the Many-Faced God

We are fascinated by death. The same obsessive, primal animus that has us relentlessly hurtling into bottomless caves, abyssal ocean depths, and the vast expanse of space makes no exceptions for what might be the greatest mystery of all. Death is all-consuming, unknowable, and inevitable; it's our very first eldritch horror, and it has haunted the human animal like nothing else.

We think about it so much that it turns up over and over again in the stories we tell ourselves. Death appears as an entity in our myths, legends, and folktales, reflecting our numerous and spirited attempts at putting a name and face to something that is ultimately incomprehensible. In these tales, death is variously a threat, an emissary, a beast to vanquish, a force to be appeased, or just a guy clocking in to carry out his cosmic nine-to-five.

The Grim Reaper

The Grim Reaper is arguably one of the most globally recognizable personifications of death. Coming from a long line of animated European skeletons, he emerged in his current form in fourteenth-century Europe,[14] when the Black Death was making its way across the continent, killing an estimated 30 to 50 percent of the population.[15] He looks appropriately horrifying for an era marked by so much trauma and death: Clad in black, he's armed with a farmer's scythe, used to reap mortal souls instead of grain.

Santa Muerte

Santa Muerte, on the other hand, is much more personable. She is worshipped as a saint throughout Mexico and its international diaspora, and her popularity among those who live in close proximity to violence has been much publicized. She counts prison guards, police officers, and narcotraffickers among her devotees. But her reputation as an impartial protector and intercessor has also made her much beloved among the old and the sick, as well as those who operate in and around the margins of conservative Catholic and societal convention. People from all walks of life set up public altars and leave offerings at her feet in the hope that she will spare them or grant them a peaceful death. ¡Viva la muerte![16]

Yama

Yama, as he appears in Hindu, Buddhist, and Chinese mythos, is the god of death, ghosts, and karmic justice. According to hymns in the Hindu Rig-Veda, he was the first being to die, establishing an underworld that he would come to rule over and blazing a path for humanity to follow. There, he serves as a guide, guardian, and judge, presiding over the deceased as the impartial Dharmaraja—the lord of the law, dishing out punishments and rewards to those who deserve them.[17]

Osiris

Like Yama, the ancient Egyptian god Osiris presided over the dead as a benevolent lord and judge. But he was also, seemingly paradoxically, the god of life, fertility, and agriculture. The story of his murder, dismemberment, and subsequent resurrection in the much-beloved myth of Osiris describes him as the first entity to be mummified, cementing him as both the god of death and the being who triumphed over it. In time, his mythological death and rebirth came to be associated with the annual inundation of the Nile River, upon which every facet of ancient Egyptian life hinged.[18]

The Coyote and the Raven

The Coyote and the Raven are two common recurring characters throughout various Native American storytelling traditions describing the origin of death. Depending on the teller, one animal is sometimes swapped out for another, but the story frequently unfolds as a debate between two parties: One side wishes for mankind to be immortal, while the other wishes for mankind to die. In one version of the story (as told by the Nlaka'pamux), the Raven argues in favor of death because he thinks that there would otherwise be too many people around, and because he wishes to feed on the dead's corpses. The Coyote, on the other hand, asserts that death should be akin to sleep. The Raven wins, but his daughter is the first to die. Distraught, he tries to alter the outcome, but the Coyote—ever the trickster—refuses.[19]

The D-Word

Death might be a familiar figure in our myths and legends, but that doesn't necessarily mean we want him at our doorstep. Today, many of us talk around the subject of death, obscuring it with euphemisms and metaphors, hiding it from our children, and putting off important conversations with friends and family until it's too late. Our fascination with death is inextricably tied to our fear of it.

We may all have differing opinions regarding the spiritual finality of death, but the permanent loss of a loved one is something we find universally awful. For many of us, death (especially one that is unexpected, sudden, or violent) is the worst kind of misfortune. In the face of such horrifying uncertainty, we often turn to little rituals known as superstitions, which are defined in the dictionary as "beliefs or practices stemming from a combination of ignorance, fear, and a dash of magical thinking."[20] While superstitious thinking is generally dismissed as irrational or nonsensical by skeptics, it's important to note that wanting some measure of control over the randomized pachinko machine of horrors that is life and death is by no means a revolutionary concept. Whether you call it karma or divine judgment, the idea that how we choose to live out our time here on earth directly impacts the kind of afterlife we'll be saddled with is a central tenet of most major religions. The difference is that while our religions and cultural narratives work to demystify death by giving it a name, superstition attempts to keep it at bay for as long as humanly possible. Both serve to alleviate a collective anxiety born of uncertainty.

Number Four

Numerical superstitions abound, but perhaps none are more strongly embraced than those associated with the number four. In parts of East Asia, the deadly digit is conspicuously absent on license plates, tech product names, and apartment doors. This is because the Chinese language—and, by extension, the languages that borrow from it—is chock-full of homophones, and the words for "four" (*sì*) and "death" (*sǐ*) are differentiated by tone alone.

Three Knocks

According to Western superstition, hearing three knocks and finding no one at your door is a sign that someone close to you has died. In general, strange noises (such as creaking, rapping on walls, and the like) heard in succession are often taken as omens of death.[21]

Curious Coffins and Riveting Rituals

Tucking Thumbs

In Japan, some feel the compulsion to hide their thumbs in their fists when visiting a cemetery, as the Japanese word for "thumb," translated literally, means "parent finger." Tucking in your thumbs is therefore believed to protect your parents from death.[22]

Black Cats

Unfortunately for our feline friends, black cats have long been associated with witchcraft, heresy, and other evils in European folklore. According to a widely circulated story, a papal decree released in the 1200s declared the poor sods incarnations of the devil, upon which they were tossed into bonfires and culled en masse by fearful peasants. While the tale is largely apocryphal,[23] a black cat crossing one's path is still seen by some today as a sign of impending doom or imminent death.[24]

Covering Mirrors

Mirrors are sometimes covered, flipped, or turned upside down in parts of Europe, America, and Asia for a variety of reasons. Some think that the first person to see their image reflected in a mirror after a recent death is the next to go, while others believe that mirrors must be obscured to prevent confusing or trapping a deceased person's soul.[25]

Holding Your Breath

Another notable superstition throughout the Western world is that one should hold their breath when passing by a graveyard to prevent nearby spirits from entering their body. This belief likely has roots in the fact that a person's breath is often connected with the idea of the spirit. Indeed, in some languages, the words for both are one and the same (as with *ruach* in Hebrew, *pneuma* in Greek, and *spiritus* in Latin).[26]

Dead

WHAT HAPPENS TO OUR BODIES WHEN WE DIE?

"For if that last day does not occasion an entire extinction, but a change of abode only, what can be more desirable?" —CICERO

PART I

Burial

Tried and True

Let's start at the very beginning. Of humanity's many funerary customs, rituals involving the burial of our dead are some of the oldest on record. There are many reasons why they have endured for so long. For one, burials serve a very practical function: Decomposing bodies don't tend to smell very pleasant, and most of us would rather not see Meemaw's body torn to shreds by wild animals or left to rot out in the open amid the hustle and bustle of daily life. Burials also appear, at least ostensibly, logistically simple; laboriousness aside, you don't need much to bury a body beyond the dirt beneath your feet. Throughout history, burials have time and time again proved to be a convenient and sensible way to keep the dead close but out of sight.

However, the emergence of intentional burials—particularly with grave goods—hundreds of thousands of years ago signaled the start of ritual behavior that seems to transcend the practical concerns of daily life. Though it is impossible to say for certain whether burials are truly our oldest death ritual, we do know that we've been deliberately and ceremoniously burying our dead for at least a hundred thousand years. Our ancient ancestors who lived in the Qafzeh Cave of Israel's Jezreel Valley buried a child with the antlers of a fallow deer in their hands,[1] and thousands of years after that,[2] our evolutionary cousins of La Ferrassie, France, buried eight of their fellow Neanderthals alongside bone shards and pieces of stone tools.[3]

Clearly, they were onto something, because we as a species have continued this tradition across millennia practically without pause, burying our bodies in some truly unexpected places, alongside the most astounding array of treasures, and with varying degrees of ceremony and extravagance.

Curious Coffins and Riveting Rituals

Not So Different

Humans aren't the only animals that bury their dead.
Ants, termites, and bees have long been known to engage
in a behavior known as necrophoresis (from the Greek
necros, meaning "dead," and *phoresis*, meaning "transport"),
whereby dead individuals are identified and removed to
prevent the spread of pathogens. Some ant species have
specialized undertakers in charge of moving these bodies
to "graveyards" within or outside the nest, while others
have been observed burying the bodies of their nestmates
under soil or other nest materials.[4] Social animals like ele-
phants and chimpanzees have been seen piling leaves and
branches over the bodies of their kin,[5] and many display
a prolonged curiosity about, and an attachment to, the
corpses and skeletons of fallen members of their species,
often carrying or guarding their remains for days on end,
regardless of whether or not a personal relation exists.[6]

Six Feet Under

These days, bodies are usually interred in coffins. Used to hold corpses for viewing or disposition, coffins can—depending on your income bracket—take the form of anything from ornate marble sarcophagi to simple wooden boxes. While the words *casket* and *coffin* are sometimes used interchangeably, a coffin is generally taken to mean a wooden container made with six sides to form a tapered hexagon. Caskets, on the other hand, are usually uniformly rectangular.

Though the prospect of slipping into the protective confines of a coffin and drifting off into an eternal slumber may seem peaceful to some, for the good people of nineteenth-century Europe and North America, it was decidedly not so. Picture this: Cholera is sweeping through your town. Current medical knowledge is shaky at best when it comes to determining if someone is *actually* dead. You, like many of your contemporaries, are understandably horrified by the prospect of being buried alive. Edgar Allan Poe even wrote a short story about it in 1844, aptly titled "The Premature Burial." This mass hysteria eventually led to the emergence of so-called safety coffins—if tobacco smoke enemas and other increasingly creative forms of physical

torture[7] failed to reanimate the presumed dead, coffins outfitted with air tubes, bells, flags, and lights could always be counted on should a dearly departed decide to wake up. Some went a step further, commissioning vaults with spring-loaded lids. Despite there being an excess of such coffin patents, cases of accidental live burials were exceedingly rare.[8]

Speaking of burial-related misconceptions, despite what a popular euphemistic idiom suggests, corpses these days aren't usually buried six feet under. However, the practice did exist at one point and may have started as a way to keep animals and grave robbers from getting at bodies. It also could have originated with a plague outbreak in fifteenth-century England, during which the mayor of London mandated that all bodies be buried at that depth in an effort to contain the disease. Today, most graves in the United States are four to five feet deep, with a foot or two of soil piled over the burial vault or casket.[9] Many modern burials are not as permanent as one might assume. In land-scarce cities such as Hong Kong, graves are rented for twenty to thirty years before they are relinquished to other families.[10] In Singapore, rental periods are even shorter, with a set maximum of fifteen years, after which the body is exhumed and either reburied in a smaller plot or cremated and moved to a columbarium.[11]

Putting the Fun in Funeral

If you're looking for something more than a simple wooden box for your casket, perhaps you might find inspiration in the colorful coffins of the Ga people. In the Greater Accra Region of Ghana, people of influence are sometimes buried in brightly colored bespoke caskets known as okadi adekai, or fantasy coffins. Handcrafted by a small group of carpenters, these caskets are often inspired by the deceased's past professions or interests and can take on some truly fantastical shapes. Depending on its complexity, each coffin can take up to three weeks to construct. It is a challenging craft to master, and each apprentice carpenter can spend as long as four years in training. Luckily, burials in Ghana can take place almost a year after death, giving the coffin makers ample time to work.[12]

Though the use of fantasy coffins is a fairly recent development,[13] they are the spiritual successors of a much older tradition of burying chiefs and kings in decorative palanquins.[14] These palanquins were usually shaped like family symbols, which were believed to protect the dead from spirits.[15] Accompanied by musical processions, Ga funerals are lively affairs.

Curious Coffins and Riveting Rituals

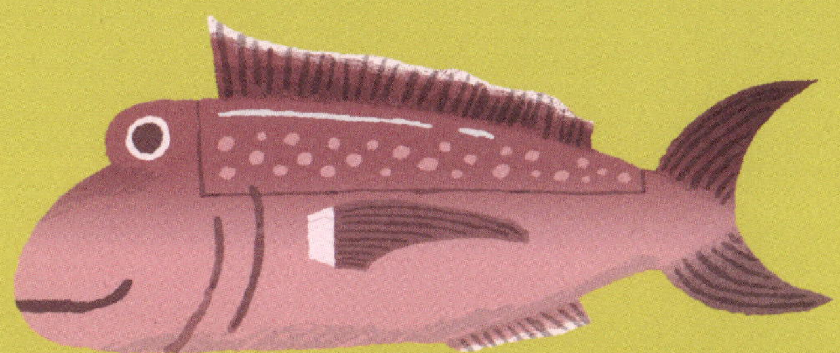

Fish

Many Ga coffins recall the deceased's former professions. For example, fishermen are sometimes buried in fish-shaped coffins.

Car

The Mercedes-Benz—for many, the ultimate symbol of modernity and wealth—is a popular choice.

Lion

Many coffins are shaped like totemic animals representative of family clans, including lions.

Plane

Some coffins are aspirational: Plane-shaped ones are always in high demand, particularly from people who've never flown.[16]

SUMBAD
LAWAGAN

High Heaven

Some are buried in interesting coffins, while others are buried in interesting places. If your coffin is going to be left somewhere (assuming it isn't pushed into a cremator and incinerated), chances are it's going into the ground. But in the mountainous municipality of Sagada, in the northern Philippines, the dead are "buried" on the sides of caves and limestone cliffs, as they have been for the last two thousand years, in what many know as hanging coffins.

There are hundreds, possibly thousands, of such coffins scattered across the valley. According to Indigenous Igorot belief, raising the dead not only keeps the corpses safe from floods and animals but also brings the deceased closer to their ancestral spirits. In preparation for death, distinguished[17] elders or members of their families carve their own coffins out of wood.[18] It is considered a sign of good luck to come into contact with a corpse's blood or bodily fluids, so after someone has died, the body is wrapped in a blanket or sheet, carried out of the home, and "passed like a ball" between relatives. In a symbolic return to the womb, the dead are interred curled up in fetal positions,[19] and their coffins are hoisted using scaffolding or lowered with vines onto natural rock shelves or poles driven into cliff faces. Over time, both the coffins and the bodies they contain degrade and merge back into their surroundings, with some even becoming entirely calcified by the limestone rocks they rest on.[20]

The ritual, once widespread across the Philippines, is now unique to the region. Sagada was mostly exempt from Spanish influence throughout the archipelago's three centuries of colonial rule, likely owing to how secluded the region is. As such, many animistic practices of yore—most rooted in the belief that animals, places, and plants are imbued with spiritual energy and hold dominion over man—were retained, despite the fact that most locals today identify as Christian. What has resulted is a unique mix of Anglican and animistic beliefs found nowhere else in the world. In the churchyard of an Anglican church (built by American missionaries in the 1890s, around the time Spain ceded control of the Philippines to the US government), bodies buried in the Christian manner are still sometimes exhumed, redressed, and reburied in the same spot during times of need, such as when a family member falls ill—a practice that borrows from Indigenous tradition. Likewise, many hanging coffins have Bible verses carved into their sides or Christian crosses laid across them.[21]

Native American Horror Story

The Igorot weren't the only ones burying their dead up high. Across the Pacific, the Sioux of the Great Plains of North America shared in this custom of aerial sepulture, interring their dead in trees or platforms up to eight feet tall. A common thread throughout Native American storytelling traditions is that death is rarely portrayed as either good or bad. Rather, it is generally presented as a natural part of life. When a member of the Sioux tribe died, they were typically wrapped in buffalo hide and bound so tight as to be waterproof. The body was then raised onto a burial scaffold tall enough to protect it from both the elements and marauding predators, then left to decompose naturally for a time before the bones were collected and buried in the ground. Bodies were often buried alongside assortments of objects that reflected the deceased's interests or skills—for example, a bow and arrows for a renowned hunter, a fleshing tool for a talented tanner, or a medicine bundle for a healer. The dead were usually buried close to settlements, where the sight of a burial scaffold silhouetted against the sky would have served as a source of comfort for the living.[22]

Of course, no discussion about Native American burials would be complete without addressing the violence that has been wrought upon them for centuries. The Indigenous dead across North America have had their remains desecrated by museums, anthropologists, and private collectors looking to expand their collections of curiosities. Bodies and the objects with which they were buried have been looted from graves, battlefields, and burial mounds to be relocated, studied, and displayed without any input from their respective tribes. These acts of violence stretch all the way back to the 1600s, when the Pilgrims pillaged the Nauset dead, and the head of Wampanoag chief Metacomet was put on a pike and displayed on Burial Hill in Plymouth, Massachusetts, for two decades. The desecration of burial sites peaked in the nineteenth century; the forced relocation of remains found interred in a twenty-five-hundred-year-old burial mound at Burr's Hill, Rhode Island, to make way for a railroad in 1851 was just one of the many horrors committed.[23]

The flagrant disregard for the Native American dead has since seeped into popular culture as the stuff of horror stories, from Stuart Rosenberg's 1979 hit, *The Amityville Horror*, to Stephen King's 1983 novel *Pet Sematary*. The disturbance of Native American burial grounds and their ancient spirits has been used to explain fictional hauntings and other supernatural goings-on so often that it has become something of a tired cliché. And it *is* horrific—not for the fictional families fleeing in fear from the vengeful ghosts they've inadvertently stirred up, but for the countless real Indigenous people who have been silenced, forced to assimilate, and robbed of their traditions, homes, and ancestral remains. It is doubly insulting that these spirits are often depicted wreaking havoc in suburban homes as if *they* were somehow the intruders.

Curious Coffins and Riveting Rituals

It was not until the passing of the Native American Graves Protection and Repatriation Act (NAGPRA) in 1990 that tribes were given the legal backing necessary to repatriate thousands of objects and human remains from federal organizations and museum collections.[24] After more than 150 years, the bodies at Burr's Hill were finally repatriated to their original sites of interment in 2017.

Grave Injustice

But the fight for total repatriation rages on. At the end of 2023, *ProPublica* reported that roughly 97,000 cultural objects remain in the possession of museums, and about 180 institutions have yet to start repatriating at all.[25] Things get even more complicated with remains that have gone missing. The period between the mid-nineteenth and twentieth centuries saw the establishment of more than six hundred government-sponsored (and often church-run) boarding schools across the United States and Canada.[26] Countless children, some as young as four, were coerced or forcibly taken miles and miles away from their families and homes to attend these institutions. There, they found themselves exploited for labor, brutally beaten for speaking in their native tongues, subjected to all kinds of physical and sexual abuse, and exposed to deadly diseases like influenza and tuberculosis (to which the students, often already weakened by malnourishment, had little resistance). Many never returned home. One report estimates that over five hundred deaths occurred at just nineteen of these schools across the United States; the actual number is likely far higher, potentially ranging from a couple thousand to tens of thousands. A number of these children were found buried in unmarked or makeshift graves with no regard for the traditional customs of their tribes, and far from the communities that mourned them.[27] Today, Native American boarding schools are seen for what they were: instruments of cultural genocide. After inflicting more than a hundred years of trauma, the US government finally issued a formal apology in 2009 for "the forcible removal of Native children from their families to far-away boarding schools where their Native practices and languages were degraded and forbidden." In 2016, the remains buried at the Carlisle Indian Industrial School (the first Native boarding school to be established in the United States) began to be repatriated to their respective tribes. As of 2024, repatriation is ongoing.[28] Many tribes have since turned to using ground-penetrating technology to find their missing dead, but for the survivors of this atrocity, the long road to healing has only just begun.

Of Grief and Gods

Burials were serious business for the ancient Greeks. More than a manifestation of grief, failure to bury a corpse was considered not only a massive insult to human dignity but also a big fat middle finger to the gods. In fact, denying someone a proper burial was considered so egregious that it was only reserved for the worst criminals, and failing to properly bury fallen soldiers—friend or foe—was a crime punishable by death.[29] The idea that death was impure and generally repulsive to the gods was pervasive throughout the Hellenic world, and death was strictly prohibited in holy places such as temples and the island of Delos—where, according to Thucydides, "all the tombs of those who had died . . . were dug up, and it was proclaimed that in future, no deaths or births were to be allowed on [Delos]; those who were about to die or give birth were to be carried across to Rhenea."[30] A death at home meant that immediate family members, water, and even fireplaces were automatically contaminated, and a death in the street often called for the decontamination of entire city zones.[31]

At the moment of death, the spirit was believed to leave the body via the mouth or an open war wound,[32] after which preparations for burial would begin. Burials were primarily conducted by close female relatives in three parts: the prothesis, the ekphora, and the burial.[33]

The graves of those who could afford it were marked with funerary statues and marble stelae decorated with verses. Some show scenes from the deceased's life, carved in relief. Though many of us associate ancient Greece with white marble, these statues and stelae were, in fact, vibrantly painted in their day.[34]

The Prothesis (Laying Out of the Body)

By law, the body had to be prepared indoors (usually in the home of the deceased), where it was washed, anointed, and clothed in red or white. The body was then laid out so that friends and family could pay their respects. Traditionally, men approached the corpse with their right hands raised, while women were expected to beat their heads and breasts in a show of grief.

The Ekphora (Funeral Procession)

A horse- or mule-drawn cart typically brought the corpse to its final resting place outside the city walls before daybreak. Main roads were avoided, and law required that the body be covered by a cloth, exposing nothing but the face.

The Burial

Most early burials didn't involve a ton of grave goods, but later burials saw the emergence of new traditions, such as that of leaving a coin, or obol, in the mouth of the deceased as a fee for Charon, the ferryman who carried the souls of the departed across the river Styx to the land of the dead.

A Traveler's Guide to Hades

Like many other peoples, the ancient Greeks believed that death was not the end but, rather, the start of something new: an afterlife invisible to the living, located in the dark, dank, and generally depressing otherworld known as Hades. Here, countless drifting spirits of the dead, known as shades, are ruled over by the eponymous god of the dead; his wife, Persephone; and the three-headed Cerberus. Though Hades himself wasn't typically portrayed as a judge or torturer, many Greeks believed him to be stern and pitiless, unmoved by prayer or sacrifice—not unlike death itself. Interpretations of the Greek afterworld diverged and evolved across different sources through the ages, but several places recur in the canon of ancient Greek literature.[35]

Oceanus, the River that Encircles the World

Homer lays out several routes to Hades in the *Odyssey*: You could make your way in through a system of dark subterranean passages, or you could sail west and over the edge of Oceanus, the world-ocean that marks the boundary between the living and the dead.

The River Styx

Upon arrival, you'll find that it is impossible to cross the Styx (arguably the most famous of Hades's many rivers) if your body hasn't already been buried, so make sure you've got that sorted out before attempting to step onto Charon's ferry.

Elysium, or the Isles of the Blessed

According to both Homer and Hesiod, you can find Elysium on the western edge of the earth on the banks of Oceanus. Here, in this beautiful, sunlit paradise, heroes of legend enjoy a life of pleasure without toil for all eternity. Early authors posited that only those favored by the gods could enter Elysium, but by the time of Pindar (in and around the sixth century CE) it had become an achievable goal for all who lived honorably.[36]

The Asphodel Fields

The neutral domain of ordinary or unexceptional souls, which is where most people end up. An average place for average people. Aim higher!

Tartarus

A dark abyss of torment and suffering that Homer describes as being "as far beneath Hades as heaven is above earth." Tartarus is home to most of the Titans deposed by the Olympians, as well as to other esteemed individuals, like King Tantalus, who killed his son and tried to feed him to the gods as a test of their omniscience. For this tomfoolery, he was sentenced to an eternity of frustration, surrounded by water he could not drink and fruit he could not touch. In Tartarus, the wicked receive their just deserts.

Curious Coffins and Riveting Rituals

OCEANUS
THE RIVER STYX
THE ASPHODEL FIELDS
ELYSIUM
TARTARUS

Stairway to Heaven

"Blessed are the pure in heart, for they shall see God." —Matthew 5:8

Many cultures possess some notion of an afterlife, but there is perhaps no image more ubiquitous than that of a Christian heaven and hell.

Christianity counts among its adherents close to 2.4 billion people across the globe—that's more than a third of the world's entire population.[37] It splits off further into smaller denominations[38] that vary in terms of theological doctrine, history, organization, leadership, and, naturally, funerary traditions. However, all Christians are more or less united in their belief about, and reverence for, the life, death, and resurrection of Jesus Christ, whose teachings are inextricably linked with the way they live and die.

The Bible tells of Jesus's sacrifice to atone for humanity's sins; his subsequent cave burial, for which he was wrapped in linen and spices; and his miraculous resurrection three days later, victorious over both sin and mortality. Early Christians emulated his interment, adhering to the Jewish ban on cremations. Keeping the body whole in death was paramount, not only out of respect for the sanctity of one's body as a "temple of the Holy Spirit"[39] but also, more importantly, due to the widespread belief in bodily resurrection come Judgment Day.

Ultimately, the hope was that one's soul would be judged righteous, penitent, and faithful enough to enter heaven—a realm of endless joy, feasts, and song where some believe the blessed dead dwell for all eternity. Other denominations (such as Roman Catholicism) view heaven as a kind of otherworldly waiting room where souls reside until the Last Judgment. On that day, one's spirit is reunited with their mortal body and, if deemed worthy, left to a future of everlasting bliss—incorruptible, whole, and untainted by sin.[40]

Highway to Hell

"But as for the cowardly, the faithless, the detestable, as for murderers, the sexually immoral, sorcerers, idolaters, and all liars, their portion will be in the lake that burns with fire and sulfur, which is the second death." —Revelation 21:8

On the flip side, most Christians believe that if someone is found evil and unrepentant, their soul is punished in hell—a fiery realm of eternal torment. Opinions as to whether it's a real place or simply a tortured state of mind tend to vary, but that hasn't stopped writers and artists across the ages from speculating. In perhaps the most famous example—*The Divine Comedy*, Italian poet Dante Alighieri's epic allegorical masterpiece about finding God— hell is described as a funnel with nine rings that descend into the center of the earth. It is essentially a vast, meticulously organized torture complex where punishments are meted out systematically according to the nature of one's sins. The lustful are whipped about by violent winds symbolic of their restlessness, gluttons are forced to lie in a vile muck representative of their overindulgence, and the treacherous are doomed to spend eternity frozen in an icy lake. In Dante's *Inferno*, you get what's coming to you.[41]

Some denominations (such as Catholicism) also believe in a middle state: purgatory, a place where those who die in God's grace but are still tainted with sin go to be purified. It's seen as a realm where temporal punishments are dealt so that one may achieve the required level of holiness needed to enter heaven.

All of this is to say that in Christianity, one's mortal life is inextricably linked to not just the promise of glory but the fear of damnation of the immortal soul. However, Christians—especially the rich and powerful—have found ways to reduce the amount of punishment they have to endure for their sins. Sure, you can live a life of compassion and faithfulness, as the Bible preaches, but you can also perform acts known as indulgences to fast-track your journey to the good place. One of the first significant acts of penance occurred in 1095, when Pope Urban II remitted participants of the Crusades who were willing to confess their sins.[42] Since then, countless people have engaged in religious fasting, pilgrimages, prayer, and acts of charity in the name of securing eternal salvation or reducing one's time in purgatory.

A Dying Trade

If all of that sounds like too much of a hassle, one can always outsource the work. From the seventeenth to nineteenth century, sin-eaters were a common sight at Welsh funerals, present in even the most remote villages across the Welsh Marches. They were often poor and desperate outcasts who were paid to consume bread and beer that had supposedly soaked up the evils of the deceased after being placed near the bodies for extended periods of time. The platters and jugs were then burned, marking the successful transfer of sins. Despite serving an important social function, sin-eaters were frequently ostracized within their communities for their association with death and evil.[43]

Turn Your Face Toward the House of God

Like Christians, followers of Islam also observe strict funerary protocols as dictated by their faith. Unlike the Bible, however, the Quran makes little mention of proper burial rites. Instead, this custom is detailed in hadiths, a narrative record of the words, actions, and teachings of the Prophet Muhammad, collectively known as sunna—"the way of the Prophet"—that serve as an important source of religious and moral guidance. As such, of the roughly two billion Muslims worldwide,[44] most are united in their belief that the body should never be mutilated by way of cremation or embalming; rather, it should be buried as soon as possible after death—preferably within the same day.[45] This custom is baked into Islamic law and pops up in several hadiths and other important texts authored by prominent medieval Islamic thinkers and other spiritual leaders. This ritual is so universal among Muslims that archaeologists have found bodies correctly dressed and oriented from the Middle East to as far west as Nîmes in the South of France.[46]

In preparation for inhumation, the body is ritually washed and enshrouded in white cloth through a process known as ghusl. This is performed by respected elders or family members of the same sex as the deceased, who handle the body in such a way that it is never indecently exposed. When this is done, the wrapped body of the dead is traditionally interred without a coffin with the body laid on its side toward the qibla—the direction of the holy city of Mecca, toward which Muslims pray five times a day.

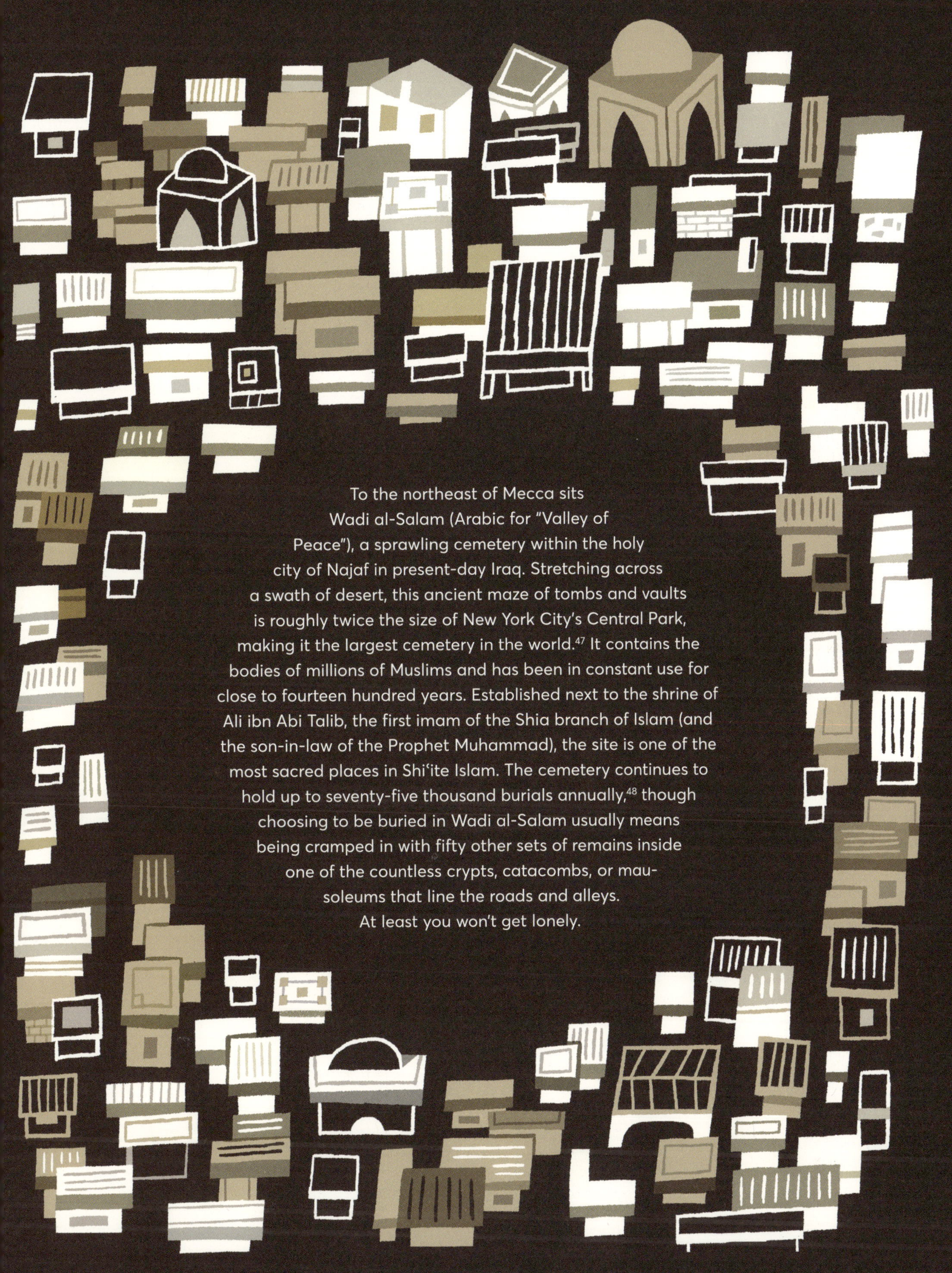

To the northeast of Mecca sits
Wadi al-Salam (Arabic for "Valley of
Peace"), a sprawling cemetery within the holy
city of Najaf in present-day Iraq. Stretching across
a swath of desert, this ancient maze of tombs and vaults
is roughly twice the size of New York City's Central Park,
making it the largest cemetery in the world.[47] It contains the
bodies of millions of Muslims and has been in constant use for
close to fourteen hundred years. Established next to the shrine of
Ali ibn Abi Talib, the first imam of the Shia branch of Islam (and
the son-in-law of the Prophet Muhammad), the site is one of the
most sacred places in Shi'ite Islam. The cemetery continues to
hold up to seventy-five thousand burials annually,[48] though
choosing to be buried in Wadi al-Salam usually means
being cramped in with fifty other sets of remains inside
one of the countless crypts, catacombs, or mausoleums that line the roads and alleys.
At least you won't get lonely.

War and Peace

On the other end of the modest-to-ostentatious burial spectrum, we have the oft-elaborate tomb structures of rulers and royalty. From the sculpted tombs of English monarchs at Westminster Abbey to the dynastic necropolises of Egypt and Ur (present-day Iraq), the idea that those at the highest levels of society should be interred in a manner befitting their importance in life is one shared across many different cultures. In addition to being buried in places and structures that were both imposing and culturally significant, people of importance were usually accompanied into the afterlife by veritable mountains of grave goods, including precious stones, weapons, clothing, furniture, and even subsidiary graves containing the bodies of servants, wives, and concubines.

Of these monumental burial sites, there are perhaps few as impressive as Qin Shi Huang's city-size mausoleum. In 1974, a group of farmers sinking a well near the northern foot of Mount Li, just outside the city of Xi'an, accidentally unearthed a life-size terra-cotta statue. What they had stumbled upon was the first of more than eight thousand stone warriors buried in a funerary complex spanning over twenty square miles, making it one of the largest tomb complexes in the world, alongside the tomb of Emperor Nintoku in Japan and the Pyramid of Khufu in Egypt. Fitting, perhaps, for the man who unified all seven warring kingdoms under one throne, introduced a standardized system of writing and currency, and masterminded the Great Wall of China.

Construction on this massive three-story subterranean city started during the emperor's lifetime in 246 BCE and continued without pause until he died in 210 BCE. More than seven hundred thousand laborers and craftsmen from all corners of the empire participated in this colossal undertaking.[49] The mausoleum itself is a scaled-down replica of the emperor's palatial complex in the then capital of Xianyang and contains a staggering amount of grave goods. Complete with weapons, chariots, terra-cotta horses, and bronze funerary carts, the mausoleum reflects that the emperor—who was reportedly so terrified of dying that he repeatedly searched for elixirs of longevity throughout his reign—spared no expense in ensuring that his final resting place was equipped with everything he could possibly need in the afterlife. It is, of course, most known for the army of terra-cotta warriors, which have stood guard over the emperor's massive pyramidal tomb in the middle of the complex

Curious Coffins and Riveting Rituals

for more than two thousand years. Positioned by rank
(and dressed accordingly),[50] the lined statues display an incredible amount of variation in both their
expressions and their facial features. Though pieces
of armor and dress recur, each head is unique—all
the way down to their earlobes, of which no two
pairs are alike.[51] The warriors are joined by a contin-
gent of entertainers, including jugglers, strongmen,
and acrobats. All the statues were originally brightly
painted, but much of that paint has since chipped off.
The emperor's actual tomb is too fragile to be excavated and has thus remained sealed,[52] but if reports
by second-century BCE historian Sima Qian are to be
believed, it is filled with "models of palaces, pavilions
and offices as well as fine vessels, precious stones and
rarities," in addition to channels of mercury representing the region's rivers and streams.[53]

Following the collapse of the Qin dynasty in 206 BCE,
the practice of interring stone warriors with the dead
passed on to the Han,[54] albeit on a much smaller scale.
Opinions about China's first emperor may have fallen
on a spectrum from effective to tyrannical, but never
let it be said that he was an easy act to follow.

The Final Voyage

Contrary to the popular image of a burning ship set adrift on the waves, archaeological evidence shows that sea burials were probably not representative of the average Viking funeral—although to call any one ritual representative of an "average" Viking funeral would be a bit of a misnomer, given the sheer diversity of customs practiced among the different ethnic, cultural, and political groups active at the time.

What we now call the Viking Age refers to a period in Scandinavian history that spanned from 800 to 1050 CE[55] across not only present-day Denmark, Norway, and Sweden but also swaths of Europe. During this time, Norsemen traded, settled, and raided. Specific rituals varied from one settlement to the next, but generally speaking, Vikings practiced both cremation and burial, with the latter being comparatively rarer.[56]

Like the ancient Greeks, Norse pagans believed in an afterlife spread across several different realms.[57] It was thought that you'd be able to bring whatever you were cremated or buried with into the hereafter, so grave goods were commonplace. As with any hierarchical society, not all were equal in death; children, slaves, and the very poor rarely show up in burial records, so much of what we know about the period has been gleaned from the remains of the very rich.[58] People of importance were often cremated and then interred in graves or mounds of dirt and stones known as tumuli, which could reach up to twenty-three feet in diameter and over fifty feet in height.[59] But even these monstrous mounds pale in comparison to the crown jewel of Viking burial rites: ship burials.

Curious Coffins and Riveting Rituals

A Quick Primer on the Norse Afterlives

Hel

A cold, dark, and damp land of the dead ruled by a being of the same name and open to men and women alike. Famous residents in this subterranean realm include the Norse god Baldr and the Valkyrie queen Brynhildr.

Sessrúmnir

The beautiful hall of Freyja, the Norse goddess of love and war, stands in Fólkvangr, a meadow that houses half of those slain in battle.

Valhalla, or Valhöll

The other half of the slain go to the legendary great hall of corpses in Asgard, where fallen warriors of great prowess feast and fight for all eternity in the presence of Odin, king of the gods. According to Norse legend, the slain were led to Valhalla by the Valkyries,[60] Odin's immortal messengers, responsible for choosing who lived and died in battle.

The Oseberg Ship

For the most famous and complete ship graves, we must travel to Norway. Discovered on a farm in 1904, the Oseberg ship is a remarkably well-preserved grave dating back to 820 CE. It contains the remains of two women—one who died in her fifties and another who died in her sixties or seventies.[61] Though their identities remain a mystery, it is clear that they were women of status, having been laid to rest in one of the richest surviving Viking graves ever found. The grave was covered by a large mound (about 145 feet wide and 20 feet high[62]), and, as noted, it is abnormally intact for its age, despite having been pillaged in the early Middle Ages. The two bodies were found buried alongside everything they could possibly need in the afterlife: the skeletons of more than ten decapitated horses, everyday objects like kitchen utensils and combs, and a slew of richly ornamented chests, textiles, sleighs, and beds.

1. This wooden bucket, complete with decorative brass fittings, contained a wooden ladle and several apples at the time of its discovery.[65]

2. It's long been speculated that the older of the two bodies belonged to Queen Åsa, the grandmother of King Harald Fairhair, but evidence is scant.

The ship itself is constructed out of decorated oak, and it was fully functional at the time it was buried, positioned with its prow facing the sea. Fully manned, it would have required thirty oarsmen to row, though it was likely used by high-ranking Norsemen as a pleasure vessel in calm waters rather than in battle. In other words, these women were buried with the Viking equivalent of a yacht.[63]

Ship burials became more widespread, with vessel sizes varying according to means and status. However, as a result of overcrowding and the spread of Christianity, they eventually waned entirely in favor of the much more sensible cist graves, which were typically rectangular stone-lined burial chambers.[64]

3 One of five wooden posts shaped like animal heads. It's unclear what function they served, but it's possible that they were made to be carried or mounted on walls.[66]

4 Though this bronze bucket handle piece found attached to the so-called Buddha bucket may bear a striking resemblance to a seated Buddha, it is in actuality a Celtic figure crafted by monks in the British Isles.[67]

5 One of four elaborately decorated sleighs found on the ship.

The Road Death Traveled

Over the ages, our dead have been laid to rest in some truly spectacular burial grounds. Next time you take a trip, why not take a brief interlude off the beaten path?

Lindholm Høje (Aalborg, Denmark)

This gigantic graveyard contains more than six hundred Germanic Iron Age and Viking graves dating from 400 to 1000 CE. Most bodies were cremated on location (though some were also inhumed), and the site is renowned for its many graves outlined with stone boats and circles.[68]

Green-Wood Cemetery (New York City, United States)

Established in 1838, Green-Wood was once the United States' second-largest tourist attraction (right behind Niagara Falls). It is known for its incredible collection of outdoor funerary art and lush natural beauty, and its popularity spurred the creation of New York City's Central and Prospect Parks. Famous residents include Leonard Bernstein, Horace Greeley, and Jean-Michel Basquiat.[69]

Père Lachaise Cemetery (Paris, France)

This is the biggest cemetery in Paris and the most visited necropolis in the world. Opened by order of Napoléon Bonaparte in 1804, it signaled a revolutionary shift away from burying the dead within city limits. As a nondenominational burial site, it counts among its inhabitants legends such as Edith Piaf, Frédéric Chopin, and Oscar Wilde.[70]

The Merry Cemetery
(Săpânţa, Romania)

Tucked away in a small northern Romanian town at
the Church of the Assumption, the Merry Cemetery
is so named for the hundreds of brightly colored
grave markers that sit within its confines, all pains-
takingly handcrafted over a period of forty years by
wood sculptor Stan Ioan Pătraș and tailored to each
deceased individual.[71]

Okunoin Cemetery (Mount Kōya, Japan)

Nestled within a sprawling temple complex containing
the mausoleum of famed Buddhist leader Kōbō Daishi
(Kūkai), Okunoin is the largest cemetery in Japan. It's also
famous for its statues of Jizo, a bodhisattva venerated as
a protector of travelers, children, and women in childbirth,
as well as for its Hall of Lamps, which contains more than
ten thousand lanterns that are kept eternally lit.[72]

The Pagoda Forest
(Henan Province, China)

Located just west of the Shaolin Temple of Song Mountain,
this cemetery—active from 791 to 1803 CE across multiple
dynasties—contains around 250 stone and brick pagodas in
which the remains of eminent Buddhist monks are interred.
The size, height, and style of each pagoda is reflective of
each monk's accomplishments, virtues, and prestige.

PART II

Cremation

The Burning Question

Fire is, by nature, transformative; it is itself a constant chemical process of combustion, and things that pass through flames emerge irrevocably changed. As one of the classical elements in both the East and the West, it holds immense symbolic meaning across many different cultures. Fire is warmth, renewal, and civilization. It lights our way to progress, keeps wild animals from dragging us off into the woods, and cooks the food that sustains us. In Egyptian hieroglyphics, fire is associated with the idea of body heat, and thus with life and health;[73] in some tellings of Greek myths, Prometheus, the maker of humanity, is also the bringer of fire. Fire is life, so it seems only fitting that for many, it is central to death as well.

Cremation refers to the reduction of a dead body by burning it until all that remains is a pile of ash and bone fragments. There is no way of knowing just how old the practice really is because, unlike burials, the burning of bodies doesn't necessitate leaving something behind. Some of the oldest cremated remains we have on record belong to an adult woman, whose bones are an estimated forty thousand to forty-two thousand years old.[74] This woman—better known as Mungo Lady—was ritually buried in the Lake Mungo lunettes, which are eroded dunes that are usually crescent-shaped. More specifically, she was first cremated, and then her bones were crushed and burned again in a secondary cremation before being ceremonially covered in red ocher and laid to rest in the lunettes.[75] Cremation eventually found its footing in other parts of the world, reaching as far as Europe, where archaeologists believe people began to cremate their dead (albeit sporadically) around 3000 BCE.[76]

Europe has historically remained relatively light on cremations, except in times of plague. With the rise of Emperor Constantine I (and, with him, Catholicism), cremations in the Roman Empire dwindled from 300 CE onward and later across the rest of Europe when his successor, Charlemagne, declared the crematory customs of the defeated Saxons and other Germanic tribes heretical in the eyes of the Church.[77] Eventually, health concerns about overcrowded urban burial grounds in the late nineteenth century led many to embrace the custom, though it wouldn't be until 1963—when the Church relaxed its ban on cremation—that the practice was able to gain serious traction in the West.[78]

In the past, most cremations took place on open pyres, and this was no simple task. Up to 60 percent of the human body consists of water, and modern estimates place the amount of wood required to burn one body at a whopping five hundred kilograms (more than one thousand pounds).[79] Today, most cremations take place in specialized furnaces within specialized buildings known as crematoriums. The burnt remains are then ground up and either displayed in urns, buried, or scattered. In many urban areas, such as Tokyo and Hong Kong, land is scarce, and cremation is by far the most dominant method of body disposition. In the United States, cremations are steadily becoming more and more widespread, with the National Funeral Directors Association estimating that by 2030, up to 70 percent of Americans may opt for cremation over traditional burials.[80]

In nature, fire plays a crucial role in the cycle of life and death. Though it might seem counterintuitive, naturally occurring fires are ecologically beneficial—even necessary—to the continued survival of certain species. Forest fires provide much-needed relief from the layer of dead organic material that suffocates the soil and its inhabitants, and the nutrients that are released from the burnt remains of this layer are essential to increasing the fertility of the soil. Pine cones can only release their seeds once the pitch that covers them has been melted, and many grazers, such as bison and pronghorn, depend on the grasses and shrubs exposed by prairie fires to thrive.[81]

Likewise, for us humans, fire removes our dead to make way for the living. There is something deeply affecting about seeing a body turn to dust before your very eyes, and many communities ascribe deep cultural significance to the ritual. For many, fire represents both physical and spiritual transformation, and the totality with which it destroys the body is often understood as a force that both cleanses and renews.

Keeping Close

Although fire is very effective at destroying bodies, rarely does it annihilate them completely. After several hours of continuous incineration, the cremator or pyre typically leaves behind a pile of ashes and bone fragments. If they aren't scattered or otherwise disposed of, they're typically stored in urns and niches. Over time, we've developed some pretty nifty receptacles for keeping our disintegrated dead close by.

Etruscan Hut Urn

Urns in the shape of rectangular houses and circular huts have been found all across central and northern Italy, which in the seventh century BCE was dominated by a web of Etruscan cities. They left little in the way of writing, but a rich archaeological record exists, including several house-shaped clay and metal urns. In addition to providing valuable information about Etruscan domiciles, they also display the cross-cultural desire to provide the dead with the domestic comforts they had known in life—a tendency the ancient Egyptians and Romans also shared.

Laotian Cremation Jar from the Plain of Jars

One of the more mysterious entries in the historical record of urns is the enigmatic Plain of Jars, located in the foothills of the Xiang Khouang Plateau in Laos. The site, which spans hundreds of square miles, contains thousands of giant prehistoric stone jars that can measure up to ten feet in height and weigh several tons. Many were plundered long ago, but some still hold grave goods and human remains that were likely cremated. Their owners and makers remain a mystery to this day; local legend holds that the jars—some of them more than two thousand years old—were the drinking vessels of giants. We may never know for sure, as the area is surrounded by millions of unexploded bombs, leftovers from the United States' involvement in the Vietnam War.

Curious Coffins and Riveting Rituals

Zapotec Effigy Funerary Urn

Some urns are more figurative, like this eighteen-inch-tall ceramic urn created in the style of the pre-Columbian Zapotec civilization of Monte Albán, one of the most important archaeological sites in Mexico. It depicts a masked deity (or a man impersonating one), and it may have originally been brightly painted. On his back is an undecorated vessel believed to have once held the remains of someone important enough to be buried in one of Monte Albán's elaborate imperial tombs.

Korean Silla Urn

As Buddhism became increasingly popular in the eighth-century Korean kingdom of Silla, cremations gradually superseded tomb burials as the standard method of disposition. When the cremated remains of the dead weren't scattered on mountains and rivers, they were placed into lidded urns and buried. Urns such as this one are elaborately decorated with stamped motifs characteristic of the era.

Death Jewelry

Today, the rapid commercialization of death has opened up a whole new world of possibilities for our ashy remains. Some companies offer grieving family members the chance to compress the remains of their departed loved ones into gemlike "death beads," while others specialize in synthesizing human ashes into diamonds and other gems.

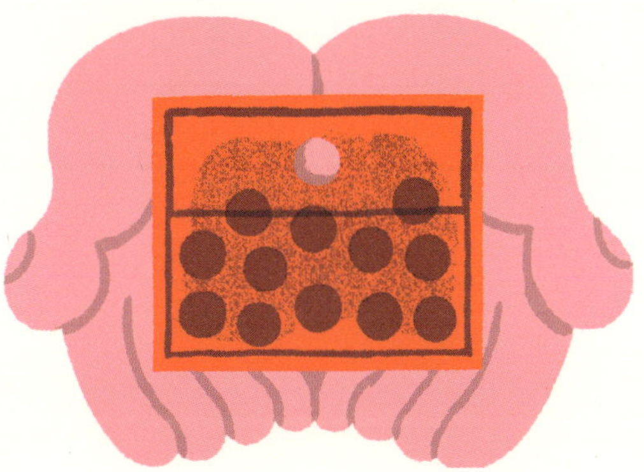

City of Death

Most modern-day cremations take place in crematoriums, where the dead are hidden away and incinerated far from the prying eyes of the living. But on the banks of India's Ganges River, the fires of a centuries-old tradition continue to burn brighter than ever.

According to Hindu belief, the souls of the deceased must be released and cleansed with fire before they can be reborn into new bodies. This endless cycle of death and rebirth, understood to be one that merely begets more suffering and pain, only ends once someone achieves moksha—the highest state of enlightenment. This is typically attained at the end of a long and arduous spiritual journey, and it is the ultimate goal for many Hindus. In India, cremations traditionally take place on open pyres located near rivers or other bodies of water. Toward the end of the cremation process, the skull of the dead is ritually pierced or broken by the lead cremator (usually the eldest son)[82] to free the spirit. Many devout Hindus have expressed disdain toward the perfunctory and impersonal nature of commercial cremation.[83] Indian-born psychologist Pittu Laungani (who was, at the time, residing in London) lamented that when the skull released the spirit in such a cremation, the spirit would remain imprisoned in the machine. It made for an akal mrityu—an unnatural death.[84]

There is, however, a way to circumvent the long road to enlightenment. Every year, millions of people make the pilgrimage to the holy city of Varanasi, one of the oldest continually inhabited cities in the world. Some, about twenty thousand annually, come to die along the banks of the Ganges, the most sacred river in India. Others come to bathe in its sacred waters, pray, and, of course, cremate their dead. On an average day, death is everywhere: Bodies are wrapped, carried down alleyways, and cremated by Dalits, members of India's lowest caste. On the ghat (stone steps leading down to the river), pyres lit by an eternal flame light up the riverbank at all hours, and the remains of the dead litter the beach opposite. Thousands of sick and elderly people can be seen milling about the streets—all of them there to die a good death. However, even the cheapest funeral pyres are out of reach for those living in abject poverty, and many spend their final days begging for alms so that they can afford their own funerals.[85] Those who aren't as close to death as they thought can spend more than ten years waiting for their time to come in charity-run hotels built to house them.[86]

Yet despite being filled with death, Varanasi is not a sad place. It is believed that if the deceased have their ashes scattered in the Ganges (so named for the goddess of salvation, Ganga), their souls will be freed from the cycle of reincarnation. The waters are considered so powerful that those who can't afford proper cremations often forgo the ritual entirely, allowing their bodies to be discarded into the river whole. For countless pilgrims who come to the city of death, there is no higher goal than achieving moksha, and no holier place to do it than Varanasi.

River of Life

Even so, Varanasi is not without its problems. Estimates vary, but roughly one hundred cremations take place across the city on any given day, each requiring massive amounts of firewood. Much of India still relies on traditional open pyres for cremation, which guzzle up anywhere from fifty to sixty million trees per year and release tons of carbon into the air.[87] And although the Ganges's namesake is venerated as a symbol of purity, the holy river is far from it. All the toxic waste generated by Varanasi's riverside cremations eventually finds its way into the Ganges, where the ashy remains resulting from this centuries-old rite intermingle with piles of floating garbage, untreated sewage, and chemical waste generated by the millions of people, factories, and farms that operate along the river basin. The result is a giant bacterial stew teeming with waterborne diseases like dysentery and cholera—one that millions continue to drink from, cook with, and bathe and swim in.[88] River cleanup is a huge undertaking that is more often than not encumbered by pushback from traditionalists, operational hiccups, and political corruption.[89] But it is an ongoing effort, bolstered by the fact that for many, this isn't just a practical problem that needs solving: It's a moral one.

Bone Voyage

In Japan, just about every person who dies is cremated. This is a fairly recent development: Burial was the primary method of disposition up until the 1930s. That said, cremation has been around since Japan's prehistoric and medieval days; the practice has its roots in Buddhist tradition and the accompanying idea of mujō, the impermanence of all things. Though cremation is not mandated by Buddhist belief, many carried it out in emulation of the Buddha's final rites.[90] On account of this, Confucian and nativist officials of the Meiji government briefly outlawed it in 1873 for being a pollutive and uncivilized custom of the past. The ensuing public outcry pitched cremation as the more practical, portable, and hygienic ritual of the future[91]—one that would aid in, not impede, the Confucian practice of ancestor worship. In an ironic twist of fate, the ban was rescinded after just two years, and cremation ended up becoming even more widely accepted among the general populace.[92]

Today, Japan's cremation rate is a staggering 99.9 percent—the highest in the world. The custom has become largely secularized, and the reason behind its dominance is mostly practical: Japan simply has no land to spare. To put it in perspective, Japan's population is about 40 percent of the United States', but the total area of all the islands in Japan combined is less than 4 percent of the United States' total area.[93] Cremation is so popular that there can be a waiting period of anywhere from a few days to several weeks if crematoriums are busy, and funeral homes can get expensive. To cope with the demand, Japan has proposed a novel solution: corpse hotels.

Part mortuaries and part guesthouses, these hotels (or itai hoteru, as they are known locally) allow grieving families to spend the night near the bodies of their loved ones as they say their final farewells. The rooms are often low-cost, open twenty-four hours a day, and fitted with small altars and platforms to hold coffins.[94] One such establishment is Lastel—as in, the last hotel a corpse will ever check into—in Yokohama. It's located near the famous ramen museum, nestled among a sea of cafés and convenience stores. After checking in, families can book two-hour-long visits, and at the push of a button, the hotel's automated coffin-retrieval system sends up the right casket from storage. In contrast to the clinical starkness of traditional morgues, the rooms in Lastel come equipped with most of the usual amenities found in a hotel or home, such as toothbrushes, TVs, and kitchens. If they so wish, families are welcome to sit and dine in the presence of their loved ones' refrigerated coffins.[95] It's a sign of changing times. In the wake of rapid industrialization, the increasingly unforgiving pace of modern life, and the gradual loosening of communal ties, Japan has shifted away from the large funerals of old, instead embracing smaller, more intimate rituals in environs such as these.

Curious Coffins and Riveting Rituals

A Bone to Pick

When it finally comes time for a loved one to be cremated, another ritual soon begins. Some families engage in a custom known as kotsuage, or "the gathering of the bones." The ashes of the dead are laid out on a table in a shūkotsu-shitsu (a room for collecting bones and ashes),[96] and the family members of the deceased are invited to pluck the bone fragments from the ashes using long chopsticks before placing them into an urn. The bones are set down in order—starting at the feet and ending with the head—so that the deceased "stands" upright in the urn.[97]

Historically, most Japanese people had (or at least aimed to have) their ashes interred in family plots to be cared for by the oldest men of the family and treated as venerable ancestors for the rest of eternity.[98] But more and more people are finding that they no longer have the time, money, or energy to perform the regular upkeep of graves, especially now that many individuals live in cities far from their ancestral hometowns.[99] Other families simply run out of descendants to take on the mantle—a real and persistent problem in light of Japan's plummeting birth rate. Regardless of the reason, people are gradually moving away from tradition, with many families turning to professionals to pulverize the remains of their dead so that the ashes can be scattered. Masuda Jūshoku (the head monk at Daitokuin Ryōgoku Ryoen) once remarked that "there are feelings that come with the bones, responsibility for the soul. Bones are real. The people who scatter the ash are trying to forget. Trying to put aside the things they don't want to think about."[100]

Into the Inferno

How Bodies Are Cremated

As cremation becomes increasingly widespread, it stands to reason that many of us will likely meet a fiery end in a crematorium. Cremation as we know it today saw its start in the second half of the nineteenth century, when urban graveyards

While the body burns in the main chamber, all the gasses and microscopic particles it produces enter a secondary chamber, where they are heated at high temperatures. This helps reduce smoke and any funky odors released during the cremation process.

First, jewelry, prosthetics, implants, and any devices containing batteries are removed from the body to prevent explosions and unwanted messes. The body is then tagged so that the remains can be identified after the cremation process.

At the end of the cremation process (which, depending on the size of the body, lasts roughly three to four hours), the remains are left to cool before being swept into a large tray.

became inundated with bodies, leading to mounting concerns about public health and disease control. The first modern crematoriums, complete with industrial furnaces pioneered by Lodovico Brunetti, opened their doors to the European public in the 1870s, with the United States following suit shortly after.[101] One hundred and fifty years later, our cremation machines still look pretty much the same. But what, exactly, happens in there?[102]

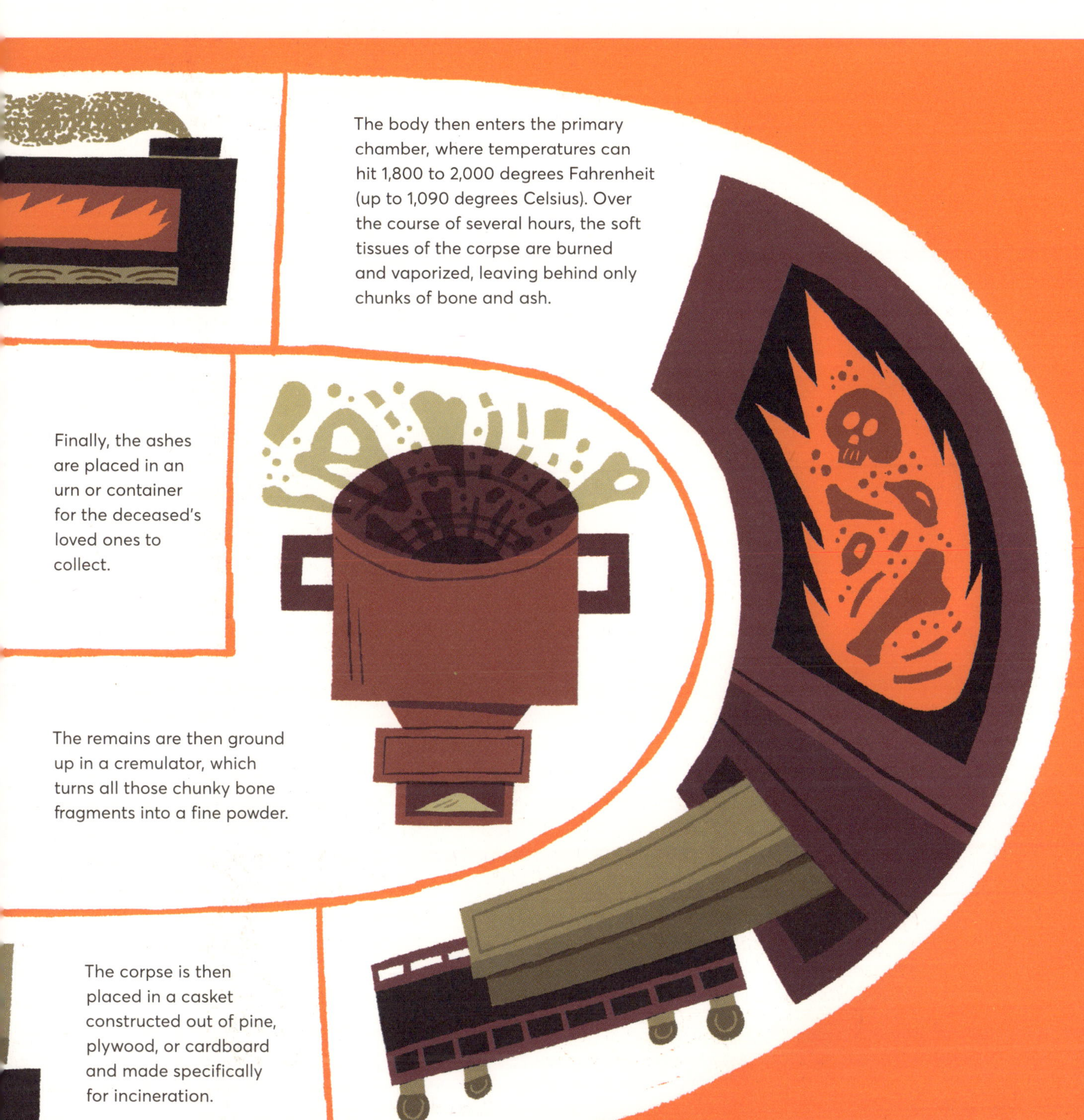

The body then enters the primary chamber, where temperatures can hit 1,800 to 2,000 degrees Fahrenheit (up to 1,090 degrees Celsius). Over the course of several hours, the soft tissues of the corpse are burned and vaporized, leaving behind only chunks of bone and ash.

Finally, the ashes are placed in an urn or container for the deceased's loved ones to collect.

The remains are then ground up in a cremulator, which turns all those chunky bone fragments into a fine powder.

The corpse is then placed in a casket constructed out of pine, plywood, or cardboard and made specifically for incineration.

PART III

Consumption

Eat, Prey, Love

So far, we've discussed burials and cremations, which are, without question, two of the most common methods of body disposition. But what if I told you there was another option?

The idea of letting our dead be taken apart, broken down, and consumed (or of being consumed ourselves) is so widely abhorred that communities the world over have devised a multitude of ways to prevent exactly that. Some may find the prospect repulsive—even offensive—but for the rest of the natural world, such is life. There is a line in one of the Vedic texts (a body of religious scriptures central to Hinduism) that reads, "Oh wonderful, oh wonderful, oh wonderful, I am food, I am food, I am food! I am an eater of food, I am an eater of food, I am an eater of food."[103] The leaf is eaten by the grasshopper, the grasshopper by the bluebird, the bluebird by the snake, and the snake by the owl. The owl dies, and its carcass slowly decomposes back into the earth, turning the ground beneath it into nutrient-rich soil from which new plant life springs, and the cycle begins anew. And on and on it goes. Humankind stands alone in breaking the flow, and by pumping our dead full of embalming fluids and burying them in impenetrable concrete vaults, we have sequestered ourselves away from the rest of nature.

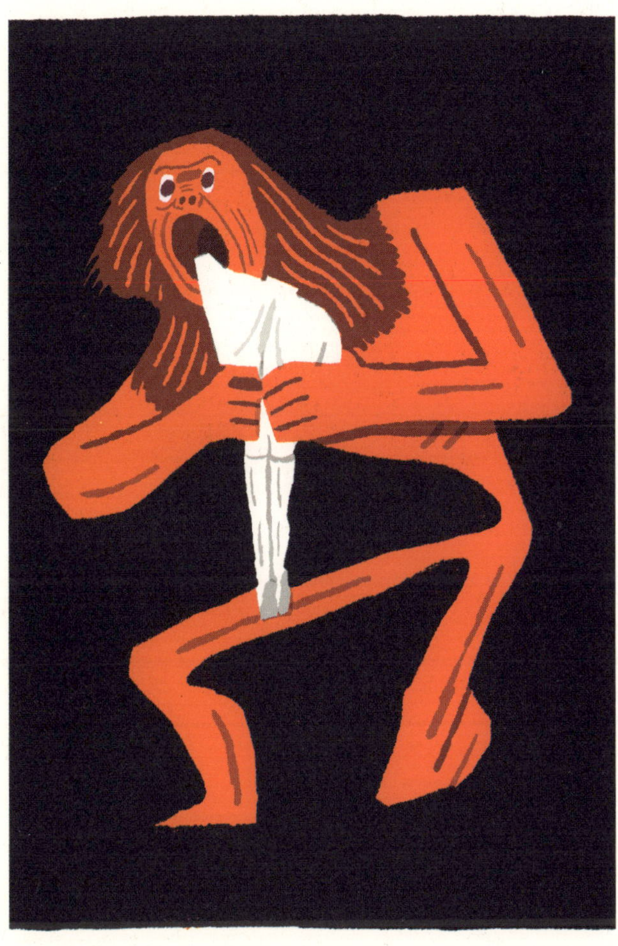

Even more disconcerting to most is the idea of the body being consumed by another human being. Cannibalism—or anthropophagy, as it's more popularly known among anthropologists—is, for many, the ultimate taboo. In the West, cannibals are the stuff of nightmares, forever typecast as the villains in true-crime documentaries and in the works of countless writers and artists (including Francisco Goya, the painter behind the frankly horrifying *Saturn Devouring His Son*) stretching back to the days of ancient Greece. But contrary to the popular image of cannibals being either deranged murderers or desperate survivalists pushed to the brink of starvation, cannibalism is surprisingly common throughout both the animal kingdom and human history, where it has occurred for a variety of reasons wholly unrelated to the need for sustenance.[104] We know that cannibalism dates as far back as the Upper Paleolithic Period, when a cache of fifteen-thousand-year-old skulls, defleshed and fashioned into cups, was found inside Gough's Cave in South West England.[105] Also found in the cave were bones, cracked open and gnawed by human teeth.[106] All across northwestern Europe, our prehistoric ancestors of the Magdalenian culture ate their dead—not for survival but, rather, for some higher symbolic purpose.[107] As practiced by Celtic Druids, cannibalism may have been part of rituals linked to agriculture and fertility.[108] Warrior peoples like the Iroquois and Aztecs consumed the flesh of their enemies as a symbolic gesture of superiority and to absorb the strength and abilities of the fallen. The belief that various parts of the body contained certain medicinal properties when ingested was so prevalent throughout medieval and early modern Europe that people from all social strata—physicians, kings, and anyone else who could afford medical care—partook.[109] A common cure for epilepsy in seventeenth-century England was the crown of a skull, ground up into a fine dust and eaten. Human blood (procured from recently executed criminals, fallen soldiers, and menstruating townsfolk) was prescribed as a cure for ailments ranging from leprosy to infertility, and it was either consumed or applied topically.[110] In premodern China,[111] devoted children would slice off parts of their flesh (usually from their thighs) to prepare a medicinal soup for parents or elders who had fallen ill as part of a ritualized practice known as gegu. In many Indigenous societies, mortuary cannibalism served an important symbolic and social function and was often not only morally acceptable but also morally obligatory. For these communities, eating their dead was an act of kindness.

Compassionate Cannibalism

In the West, cannibalism tends to conjure up horrifying images of psychosexual serial killers, starving colonists, and fairy-tale witches. It is not hard to see why; many of us have a hard time separating an individual's personhood from their flesh-and-blood body. Some believe the dead to be spiritually and physically contaminative, unfit to be laid to rest anywhere near the living, let alone *eaten*. Others find cannibalism disturbing in how seemingly counterintuitive it is to our primal, life-affirming instincts. We are, after all, the eaters of food, not food ourselves . . . right?

Unfortunately, this deep-seated disgust has been weaponized time and time again throughout history, raised as a moral argument to justify ideas of European superiority in the oppression and subjugation of countless colonized peoples. In actuality, many reports of cannibalism were of dubious veracity—at worst, outright lies used to exploit and enslave Indigenous tribes, and at best, overly sensationalized exaggerations meant to bolster the reputations of seafaring explorers.[112] In any case, we are all mired in what American anthropologist Clifford Geertz referred to as "webs of significance," wherein everything we believe—from what we consider "right" to what we think of as "normal"—is relative, ingrained in us by our cultures.[113] Although evidence of cannibalism has been found in places such as the Pacific Islands and parts of Africa and South America, it is clear that it occurs mostly within the context of ritual action.[114]

Such is the case with the Wari', an Indigenous Amazonian people who, up until the 1960s, ate their dead. Endocannibalism refers to acts of cannibalism that occur within an in-group—between, say, members of the same family or tribe. Unlike exocannibalism (in which those eaten are typically one's enemies during periods of war and strife), this usually happens in the context of mortuary cannibalism. In other words, what the Wari' practiced was a symbolic act, not one necessitated by a need for sustenance.

When someone died, relatives of the deceased gathered for the funeral and disposed of the dead the same way their ancestors had for centuries: by consuming all or most of the dead's roasted flesh and select organs, as well as ground bones on occasion, and burning the rest. As with cremation, the complete destruction of the corpse was the intended outcome. The duty of preparing and eating the corpse fell to individuals whom they considered distant relatives, usually the in-laws of the deceased. It was an act of social obligation—a kindness owed to the family into which the in-laws' child had married[115]—and it was by no stretch of the imagination a pleasant one. By the time those gathered got to eating the corpse, the body would've been stewing in the hot, muggy rainforest for several days. Eating the decomposing flesh would've been a thoroughly foul experience, and many had to take breaks to vomit before they could force themselves to continue.[116] Almost everyone was eaten, regardless of age or cause of death, and those who weren't were cremated. After the funeral, the dead person's dwelling, along with everything they ever owned, was burned to the ground.

Now, you might be asking *why*. Why eat the corpse if it was so difficult to swallow? Why eat a corpse at all? When asked by anthropologist Beth Conklin, elders who had taken part in these rituals simply replied, "Je' kwerexi" (thus was our custom).[117] The Wari', for as long as anyone could remember, had simply disposed of their dead in this manner. It was honorable and kind—something they wanted to do

Curious Coffins and Riveting Rituals

for others and something they wanted for themselves. Many also believed that since we are born from the body of a human being, we should leave the way we came. The phrase *xiram pa'* (feeling sorry for someone) was also echoed; by divvying the body up into increasingly unidentifiable parts and consuming them, the living helped assuage some of the grief felt by the community. Through cannibalism, they were systematically removing reminders of the beloved dead.[118]

Further, the idea that a body would be degraded and disrespected to the point that it was left to rot in the cold, wet ground absolutely horrified them. This unfortunately came to pass in the 1950s and '60s, when the Brazilian government made contact with the Wari', bringing with it a whole host of diseases against which they had no immunological resistance. By the time the surviving population assimilated in the early '60s, most had been coerced into burying their dead.[119] Today, the younger generation looks at mortuary cannibalism as a curious thing of the past, and it is unlikely that it will ever make a comeback. However, many of those who still remember the ritual feel distinctly that something meaningful has been lost.[120]

Circle of Life

Like Hindus, Buddhists believe in the cycle of reincarnation. Naturally, when a person dies, the body their spirit leaves behind is treated like an empty shell. However, in the cold, mountainous regions of Tibet and South Asia, wood is scarce, and the ground is hard and rocky, making burials an impossibility and cremations ridiculously expensive. As such, many locals turn to another ancient tradition: sky burials.

Despite the name, sky burials don't involve any burying. To return a body to the earth, it is taken apart by a rogyapa (as in a "breaker of bodies"), someone who systematically rends limbs from torso, hair from head, and flesh from bone. The rest of the skeleton is mixed in with tsampa, a traditional Tibetan dish made with barley flour and yak butter, and ground into a paste. The remains are then laid in a clearing or on a rock face to decompose naturally, or they are fed to vultures in one final act of charity.[121]

Nature's Undertakers

The bodies are typically fed to Himalayan vultures, which subsist entirely on carrion. In Tibetan Buddhism, the moment of death is considered crucial in determining the rebirth that is to come in the endless cycle of reincarnation known as samsara.[122] To be able to die knowing that your body will nourish another living being—and, by extension, to be able to honor this wish as a rogyapa—is considered a great gesture of compassion and virtue. Vultures are considered sacred, and it is seen as a bad omen if they choose not to eat a body. This became especially contentious following the spike in Tibetan thanatourism, when nosy tourists sometimes scared off nearby vultures when they were brought to witness parts of the ritual that not even the deceased's family members were privy to. In 2005, the Tibetan government finally passed a law limiting tourism in and around sky burial sites.[123]

Death from Above

In ancient Persia, a similar ritual was practiced by Zoroastrian Parsis, who built raised circular structures known as dakhmas, or "towers of silence," across present-day India and Iran to expose the bodies of the dead to the elements and carrion birds. The practice (known to its practitioners as dokhmenashini) stems from the belief that human and animal corpses are nasu, or unclean. To prevent corpses from contaminating the earth, fire, air, and water—considered sacred by the prophet Zarathustra and his followers—Parsis traditionally place their dead atop funeral towers following elaborate funerals. During the funerals, the corpses are customarily washed and wrapped by trained attendants. Prayers are recited, and a sacred dog is brought in to conduct the sagdid—literally "the seeing of the dog"—by glancing at the corpses.[124] The bodies are then stripped of all clothing and brought to the towers, where they remain until they are picked clean by vultures and other birds.[125]

Or that's the idea, anyway. As with Tibetan sky burials, this system of exposure hinges on the presence of scavenger birds such as kites, crows, and, most importantly, vultures—whose mystic eyes are said to aid the souls' transition into the next life.[126] The ritual has largely fallen out of use in modern times; most of the towers have been abandoned, including Yazd in central Iran, where rapid urbanization and evolving sensitivities led to the prohibition of the practice in the 1970s.[127]

Today, India—where some of these ancient dakhmas still stand hundreds of years after they were built—is the last bastion of this ancient ritual. In Mumbai, Parsis enjoy some measure of goodwill, as their forebears were responsible for building much of the city's cultural and economic wealth.[128] Here, the survival of dokhmenashini is threatened by a much bigger problem. The country that was once home to up to four hundred million vultures has since lost a staggering 99 percent of them, a majority poisoned by diclofenac, a toxic painkiller used to treat sick cattle.[129] Though the Indian government has since banned the drug and set up sanctuaries in a bid to recover its resident vulture population, many Parsis have had to resort to alternative means of corpse exposure. Solar concentrators were introduced to heat up bodies and speed up the rate of decomposition, though they can't be used on cloudy days or when it pours during the monsoon season. A job that would've taken a flock of vultures several hours can now take several weeks—something many Parsis (and their neighbors) find thoroughly disconcerting.[130]

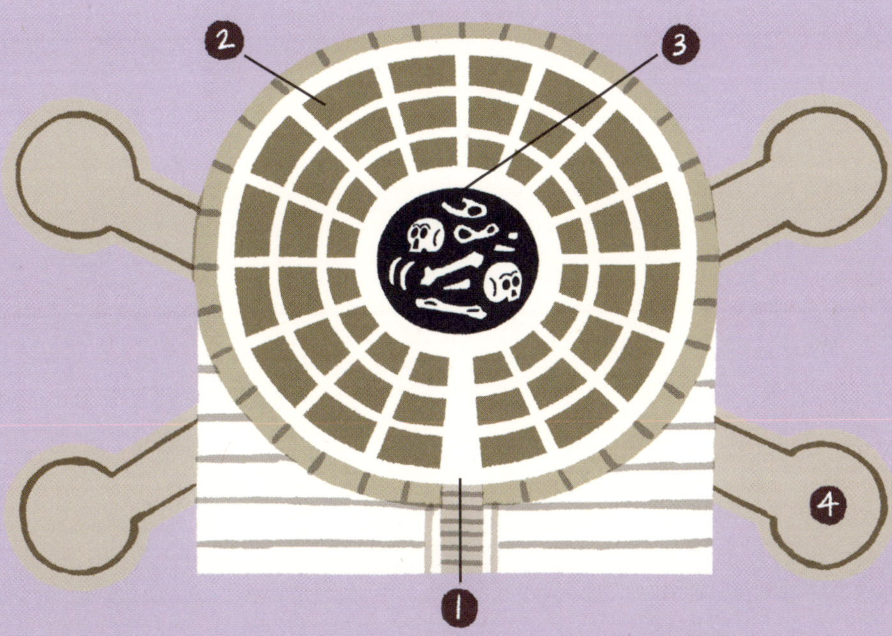

1. The average dakhma, accessible through a single door, is typically around three hundred feet tall.

2. The towers are built like large amphitheaters, complete with open tops lined with concentric stone circles. Bodies are arranged according to age and gender: men on the outer rim, women in the middle, and children in the innermost circle.

3. After a while, the bones that remain are left out to dry for a few days before they are moved to the bhandar—the 150-foot-wide well in the middle of each structure. In time, the skeletal remains of the dead crumble to dust.

4. When it rains, putrefying matter expelled by the exposed bodies makes its way through a system of underground drains connected to the central well and moves into four outer wells, each containing a thick layer of charcoal and sand.

To Be Continued

Sky burials appear to be one of the rare mortuary customs in which human bodies are allowed to participate in the natural cycle of life and death, but whether we choose to be embalmed, buried, or cremated, we are all headed the same way: What remains of our bodies will eventually be broken down and returned to the earth. This may take anywhere from a few weeks to a couple of centuries, but all the same, death marks an end to an old life, and decaying remains make way for the new.

At least, that's probably the way it should be. There was once a time when most bodies buried underground were allowed to gradually decompose into the earth. Today, the widespread use of burial vaults and embalming practices have made burials a lot less decomposition-friendly, and a lot more pollutive. According to the Green Burial Council, burials in the United States deposit up to 4.3 million gallons of embalming fluid (including about 830,000 gallons of formaldehyde), 20 million board feet of wood, 1.6 million tons of concrete, and 64,500 tons of steel into the earth. Burial vaults and caskets leach iron, copper, lead, and other metals into the soil, poisoning it even further.[131] Likewise, cremation machines typically run on a diet of natural gas, expelling billions of tons of CO_2 (along with mercury, nitrogen oxide, dioxins, and other nasty particulates) into the air and water.[132]

But as the climate crisis grows increasingly dire, more and more people have begun to embrace eco-friendlier options for mortuary disposal. According to the National Funeral Directors Association, more than half of Americans surveyed called for greener funerals, and the funeral industry answered. Today, barring state and national laws, you can have your remains entombed in an artificial reef ball, buried in a biodegradable coffin made from woven willow or bamboo, stripped of toxins by a mushroom suit, or dissolved via alkaline hydrolysis. The latter, also known as water cremation, turns you into a vat of tea-colored juice that can safely be used as fertilizer—or poured down the drain, if you so wish.[133]

You could also be turned into plant food. The term *human composting* may sound disturbing to some, but for those living on the tiny island of Lyrön, Sweden, it is the future of death. Promession, a process developed by biologist Susanne Wiigh-Mäsak, entails freezing a corpse using liquid nitrogen before shattering it into pieces. The chunks are then freeze-dried and used to fertilize a memorial tree or shrub that is planted in a churchyard or in a family's backyard.[134] Wiigh-Mäsak isn't the only one who saw in compost a vision of the future: The first person to ever compost a human body was an American by the name of Tim Evans, who in 1998 composted a body donated to a university using a mix of manure and wood shavings, commenting that this was "as close . . . as science is going to get to reincarnation."[135]

PART IV

Preservation

Chasing Immortality

Although rituals involving burial, cremation, and consumption can differ greatly, the end goal is usually the same: putting away, getting rid of, or reducing the body in some manner. Out of sight, out of mind, as the saying goes. But sometimes grief leads us down a different road. Sometimes we want our dead to stick around just a little longer.

Occasionally, nature does the job for us. Bodies left out or buried in places that are either extremely dry and hot or extremely dry and cold—think scorching deserts and subzero mountaintops—can sometimes remain shockingly well-preserved for centuries. Naturally mummified bodies have also been found in bogs, which are swamps made from decaying or decayed peat moss that contain just the right amount of acidic, oxygen-denying sludge to forestall decomposition.

The Tollund Man

Discovered in a bog just west of the town of Silkeborg, Denmark, the Tollund Man is probably the most famous bog body of them all. He died in the fifth century and lay preserved in his swampy grave, which maintained him so well that Danish authorities initially mistook him for a recent murder victim when he was found in 1950. It also turned his skin a distinctive leathery brown.[136]

The Llullaillaco Maiden

Found frozen solid near the summit of Llullaillaco (a dormant volcano on the Argentina-Chile border), the Llullaillaco Maiden was one of three Incan child sacrifices left to die atop the world's highest archaeological site some five hundred years ago. When she was found, her mouth and body still contained traces of alcohol and coca leaves, both of which would have served as powerful sedatives before she was left to die.[137]

The Salt Men of Iran

The Salt Men were a bunch of unlucky miners trapped by two separate cave-ins at the Chehrabad salt mine centuries apart (one group perished between the sixth and fourth centuries BCE, while the others died hundreds of years later between the second and sixth centuries CE).[138] The salty rock sucked the moisture out of their bodies and mummified their crushed remains.

Though some of these bodies were mummified by sheer chance (as an unintended consequence of an otherwise routine burial, for example, or because they had simply died in the right place at the right time), some of them exhibited signs of ritualistic behavior. The Llullaillaco Maiden was found fitted in a ceremonial tunic and headpiece,[139] while others, like the Tollund Man, had been deliberately laid to rest in a sleeping position.[140] It is possible that the people who inhabited these territories were cognizant of the preservative effects of their surrounding locales, depositing their dead into peat bogs, mountain caves, and shallow desert graves, then letting nature take its course, though we can't know for sure. Either way, nature doesn't always make for the most reliable mortuary assistant. Assuming that these extreme and often unusual conditions are met, the body still has to somehow avoid being eaten or destroyed by elemental damage, fungi, bacteria, and animals, making natural mummies exceedingly rare finds. Simply put, if you really wanted your dead to live forever, you had to take matters into your own hands.

And so we did. Throughout history, people from all over—from Central America to China to ancient Ethiopia—intentionally embalmed and mummified their dead using an array of spices, minerals, and later chemicals to shield bodies from the threat of decay.[141] Sometimes the entire body was preserved, as is often the case for mummified corpses; other times, only certain parts of the body were kept. The oldest artificially mummified bodies on record belong to the Chinchorro, a culture of marine hunter-gatherers who embalmed and buried their dead in the hot, arid deserts of what is now northern Chile approximately seven thousand years ago—two thousand years before the ancient Egyptians started mummifying theirs.[142] The desire to keep our dead looking as they did in life is a cross-cultural impulse, and we've been acting on it for centuries for reasons both practical and abstract. Bodies are sometimes preserved to keep them looking presentable and sanitary for use in dissections and scientific study, or in the event that they had to be moved somewhere or viewed at a later date. Other times, the dead or their parts are preserved, displayed, and kept for protection, power, or guidance.

Today, embalming is a common practice throughout the United States, and many funeral directors are legally bound by state laws to train as embalmers, even if it is never needed in practice.[143] We preserve the bodies of our dead to delay the inevitable, but nobody—and no *body*—is exempt from the ravages of time and rot. We start to decompose the second we die; our bodies undergo a process known as autolysis, wherein our cells release enzymes that literally start eating at us from the inside out.[144] No method of preservation, no matter how advanced, has so far succeeded in eliminating decomposition entirely. In other words, chasing immortality is almost certainly an exercise in futility. But when has that ever stopped us from trying?

   Curious Coffins and Riveting Rituals

Miracle Makers

In Catholicism, bodies of the exceptionally virtuous—sometimes miraculously preserved on account of their spiritual and moral incorruptibility—are believed to be imbued with mystical power. Relics, as these bodies and body parts came to be known, can be found scattered throughout Europe, encased in elaborate reliquaries, buried under altars, and venerated by people of the faith. Many of them belong to canonized saints, with some of the most popular being persecuted martyrs. In their sainthood, they achieved one of the main goals sought by all Christendom: the privilege of ascending straight up to heaven without having to spend any time in the limbo of purgatory or face the fiery torments of hell. Instead, they were believed to dwell alongside God, where they assisted their earthly beneficiaries as the most powerful of intercessors. Praying to (or, better yet, touching) one of these saintly relics was considered the most direct route to accessing the holy miracles made possible by God.[145]

The term *relic* refers to a broad classification of ritual objects that vary in spiritual potency depending on what they are. Objects taken directly from the events of Christ's life (such as bits of the holy cross) or the physical remains of a saint reign supreme—even more so if the saved body part was tied in some way to the saint's celebrity, such as the head of a theologian or the right hand of a king. Objects that were used by the saint or that came into contact with another important relic were also considered sacred, albeit to a lesser degree. All the same, relics became highly sought-after in the Middle Ages as markers of prestige and guardians against disease and disaster. In 787, after the Second Council of Nicaea passed into law the requirement that every church altar have a relic, these objects became necessary for the continued survival of a church.[146] In an era marked by widespread illiteracy, the immediacy of saintly relics made God's presence both tangible and easily identifiable,

and relics became local and national attractions, worshipped by kings and serfs alike.[147] They were the linchpins of medieval life and faith: Cathedrals sprang up to house them, becoming places of pilgrimage and commerce that allowed for the establishment of countless cities and towns. And if you couldn't make it to these churches, they would sometimes come to you via church processions.

And as with anything high in value and low in supply, fakes and frauds abound. Counterfeit relics were frequently exposed in the Middle Ages, and the Church conducted systematic reviews of each claim to fame; panels of officials were involved in investigations, witnesses were interviewed, and spiritual proof was gathered before a relic was declared authentic.[148] But more than a few slipped through the cracks. The bones of Saint Rosalia—the patron saint of Palermo, Sicily, who died a hermit in 1160 after purportedly being led to a cave by a pair of angels—were exposed by nineteenth-century naturalist William Buckland as the remains of a goat.[149] John the Baptist's holy head has popped up in the Great Mosque of Damascus, the Amiens Cathedral in northern France, the Basilica of San Silvestro in Capite, and again in a collection owned by Duke Wilhelm V of Bavaria.[150] Unless he secretly lived life with more than one head, somebody's lying.

IN SAINT STEPHEN'S BASILICA IN
BUDAPEST,   HUNGARY

THE RIGHT HAND OF SAINT STEPHEN

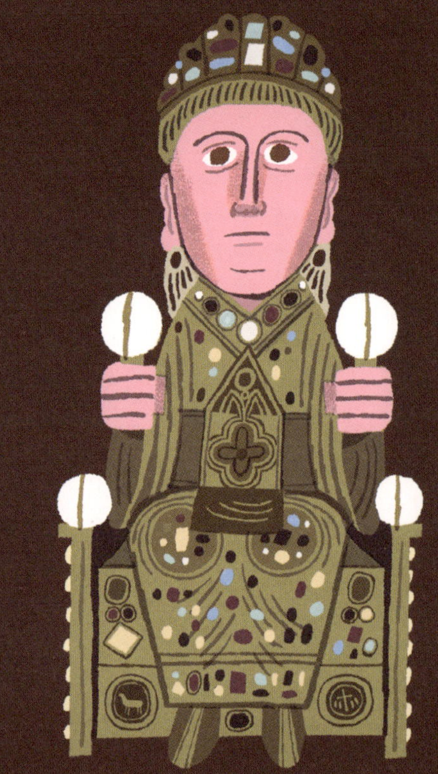

SAINTE FOY'S SKULL

IN THE CHURCH OF SAINTE-FOY
IN CONQUES, FRANCE

IN THE CATHEDRAL OF
THE ASSUMPTION
OF MARY
IN NAPLES,
ITALY

THE BLOOD
OF SAINT
JANUARIUS

THE HEAD OF JOHN THE BAPTIST

IN THE AMIENS CATHEDRAL
IN AMIENS, FRANCE

SAINT NICHOLAS'S FINGER

SAINT ANTHONY'S JAWBONE
IN SAINT ANTHONY'S BASILICA IN PADUA, ITALY

The Life and Times of Saint Catherine

1 Set in two ornate reliquaries in the Basilica of San Domenico in Siena, Italy, are the severed head and right thumb of Saint Catherine, a fourteenth-century nun, writer, and mystic.

2 Like most saints, she experienced many miracles in her lifetime, such as levitating during prayer and seeing holy visions of Jesus Christ, the Virgin Mary, and other saints—the first of which occurred when she was just five or six years old. She swore a vow of chastity when she was seven and, to the dismay of her parents, finally joined the Dominican Tertiary at sixteen.

3 At the age of twenty-eight, Catherine entered into a "mystical marriage" with Jesus and received, among other miracles, stigmata—the wounds of the crucified Jesus Christ—on her hands and feet. As the story goes, she also received a call from Christ to leave her life of solitude and tend to the sick and impoverished.

4 The saint would go on to devote the rest of her life to the poor and ailing, and when she wasn't helping the less fortunate, she was writing. A prolific writer, she penned an extensive collection of letters to popes, monarchs, and laypeople. These missives, through which she preached the will of God, were incredibly influential both during and after her life.[151]

5 Catherine died in Rome at the age of thirty-three after years of rigorous fasting, and she was buried in the graveyard of the Basilica of Saint Mary of Minerva (though, for one reason or another, she was soon exhumed and buried in the church itself). The people of Siena, however, wanted their local saint back. Raymond of Capua, general of the Dominican Order and Catherine's spiritual adviser, had the saint's head detached from her body and smuggled out of Rome in a silk bag. Back in Siena, it was conveyed to the Dominican church in a procession across the city. Catherine's mother, who outlived most of her children, accompanied her daughter's head. The rest of Catherine's body remains enshrined in Rome in the Basilica of Saint Mary above Minerva.

6 The saint's fame grew quickly after her death, and she was canonized a century later in 1461. In 1970, along with Teresa of Ávila, she became one of the first women to ever be made a doctor of the church for her contributions to Catholic theology. Today, she is venerated as a patron saint of Italy, as well as of sickness, nurses, and bodily ills.

Remains to Be Seen

For many members of the Catholic or Eastern Orthodox faiths, the chance to be buried in hallowed grounds was not simply an honor, but a matter of spiritual necessity—and the churchyard was prime real estate. Churchyard burials proved so popular, in fact, that most eventually ran out of space to accommodate the constant stream of dead bodies. As such, churches began burying people in temporary graves, then digging up their bones and storing their skeletal remains in ossuaries— depositories that range from small chests to large chapels containing thousands of skeletons.

Although most of these ossuaries started out as glorified storage closets, churches eventually began installing viewing windows for interested onlookers and putting the bones on display in rooms open to the public. Today, you can find ossuaries, crypts, and charnel houses scattered across Europe, and many are home to some truly spectacular bone art. From bone sculptures to painted skulls, these macabre creations are merely the latest in a long line of bones that have been preserved and decorated—some of which date as far back as the Neolithic period. Caches of skulls coated in plaster and decorated with shells and paint to re-create human faces have been found in the Middle East, where it's possible they were used to commemorate the recent dead or venerated as ancestral figures.[152]

Needless to say, most ossuaries attached to churches probably weren't gunning to encourage ancestor worship. Rather, their skeletal collections were a kind of memento mori, a reminder that this is what awaits us all: death and anonymity in a sea of bones. Clearly, all the earthly glories in the world made no difference for these schmucks, so you'd best focus on what really matters—your faith and salvation.[153] As for how successful they were in inspiring godly contemplation, well, you'll have to judge for yourself.

The Catacombs of Paris, France

Measuring up to sixty-five feet deep and nearly two hundred miles long, the Catacombs of Paris consist of a sprawling maze of underground tunnels deep in the heart of the City of Light. This subterranean network forms one of the largest ossuaries in the world, though only a small section is open to the public. Formerly a stone quarry, the Catacombs were first used to house the dead from the now-defunct Cimetière des Saints-Innocents, once the largest cemetery in Paris. Today, it contains the bones of more than six million people (many of whom were plague victims) whose skulls have been stacked into walls that run on for miles and miles.

Hallstatt Charnel House, Austria

Nestled in the ridiculously scenic region of Austria overlooking the Alps, this subterranean charnel house is home to 610 hand-painted skulls—the largest collection anywhere in Europe. Before each skull was painted, it was first disinterred from its grave and left under the sun until all signs of decay had subsided and the bones had been bleached a pale white. It was then decorated with flowers, along with the deceased's name, birth date, and death date. By the nineteenth century, people had really started to take umbrage at the whole "anonymous dead" thing, so this was intended to make the skeletal remains of one's family easy to spot in a pile of bones. The practice began to wane in the 1960s, when the Church loosened its ban on cremation, bringing the millennia-long problem of overcrowded graveyards to a close, but you can still request to have your bones interred there.

The Sedlec Ossuary, Czech Republic

Located in the small town of Kutná Hora, this Roman Catholic chapel looks pretty unremarkable from the outside. But have a peek under the cemetery and you'll be met with bone sculptures as far as the eye can see. Here lie the bony remains of roughly sixty thousand people, many of whom were drawn to the site after a local abbot sanctified the churchyard with some dirt picked up during a thirteenth-century pilgrimage to Jerusalem. Another forty thousand or so joined the ossuary following the devastation wrought by the plague and the Crusades in the fourteenth century. Five centuries later, Czech wood-carver and carpenter František Rint was brought in to arrange the bones, transforming a not-insignificant portion of the ossuary's occupants into chalices, tableaus, and even a family crest. But his pièce de résistance is undoubtedly the bone chandelier hanging in the middle of the chapel that is said to contain every bone in the human body.

Headfirst

Catholic reliquaries aren't the only example of the dead being kept to aid the living. Human skulls are sometimes kept in the homes of the Indigenous Aymara people of Bolivia, where they are treated as beloved family members and looked upon as powerful spiritual advisers, guardians of the home, and good luck charms.

These skulls are known as ñatitas, or "little pug-nosed ones." Interestingly enough, they usually don't belong to their owners' deceased relatives or loved ones. Instead, most are obtained through medical schools, archaeological sites, and evicted cemetery plots. The fact that they frequently belong to complete strangers is of little concern, and some have even been said to alert future owners to their presence by way of dreams.[154] Every ñatita is a skull, but not every skull becomes a ñatita. Each is believed to have its own personality, and sometimes an owner can have a falling out with their ñatita. Along with these distinct personalities come distinct gifts: When writer and mortician Caitlin Doughty visited the home of Doña Ely (the keeper of several ñatitas); she was introduced to Carlito, who primarily dealt with medical problems, and Cecilia, the patron skull of university students. Ñatitas are believed to hold sway over all aspects of life: Some specialize in preventing robberies, while others are consulted primarily by bankers in need of professional guidance. All enjoy offerings of candy, soda, and fruit, left behind by their grateful followers, who come to them for wisdom and pray for their intercession.[155]

The ritual of the ñatitas persists in La Paz, despite the regional dominance of Catholicism, due to the continued effort of the Aymara people, Bolivia's second-largest Indigenous group. Skulls have a long history of ritual significance in the region; Andean[156] belief held that heads were the locus of wisdom and power, both of which could be transferred to another person so long as they had possession of said heads.[157] Trouble came when the Spaniards arrived in Bolivia in the sixteenth century, forcibly converting the country's native population to Christianity, putting those who resisted on trial for worshipping the devil, and systematically stamping out traditions rooted in Indigenous belief.[158] Up until recently, the chapel in La Paz refused to entertain Sunday festivals that celebrated ñatitas. The message was clear: Venerate the bodies of the holy dead—but do it our way.

Ideas, however, aren't so easily destroyed. In the face of discrimination and oppression, the practice simply went underground. What exists today is a kind of syncretic belief system, where normative Catholic rituals belie a not-so-subtle undercurrent of folk magic. In La Paz, portraits of the Virgin Mary hang across from private shrines, and clairvoyants such as Elizabeth "Eli" Portugal Coronez de Aduviri—the owner of a whopping seventy-three ñatitas—describe their mystical connection with the skulls as a gift from God.[159]

Thinking Ahead

Skulls are sometimes used to foretell the future. Coca leaves are placed in a skull's mouth, then chewed by a medium who makes predictions based on their sweetness. Aymaran witch doctors known as yatiri are sometimes also employed to commune with the spirits.[160]

Day of the Skulls

Ñatitas have their own holiday—the annual Fiesta de las Ñatitas. Unlike most festivals of the dead, it is held not to commemorate loved ones lost or to cope with the inevitability of death but to celebrate the bond between the skulls and their owners. In La Paz, the festival attracts huge crowds of anywhere from five thousand to ten thousand people.[161] During the festival, thousands of skulls are taken out of their homes and carefully dressed before being brought to local cemeteries in protective glass boxes or atop satin pillows. The owners pray and sing through the city's streets, putting their beloved skulls on display throughout the main cemetery, where they are serenaded and showered with offerings of coca leaves, cigarettes, and flowers.

Lending a Helping . . . Head?

Outside of the fiesta, ñatitas generally maintain a low profile. Most are kept in shrines or cabinets at home, but some are used to aid businesses and organizations. Such is the case for a pair of ñatitas kept in one of La Paz's police stations, affectionately dubbed Juanito and Juanita by detectives. They have been credited with helping to solve hundreds of cases, and officers frequently leave written requests for information on their shrines. In return for their faithful service, the skulls are offered votive candles, candy, cigarettes, and coca leaves.[162]

That's a Wrap

Chances are, the first image that leaps to mind when anyone mentions preserving human bodies is that of a mummy. And out of all the human and animal mummies that have been found across nearly all the continents of the world, the most famous are, without question, those from ancient Egypt.

The earliest prehistoric mummies were buried curled up in the sand, preserved naturally by the hot and arid climate of the Egyptian desert, where there is often no measurable rainfall. But by 2600 BCE,[163] ancient Egyptians had begun to intentionally mummify their dead in an effort to ensure that their spirits could continue on their journeys toward immortality in the afterlife. They perfected the technique over the next two thousand years until its gradual decline toward the end of the Roman era in 311 CE, with the rise of Christianity in Egypt around the fourth century BCE proving to be the final nail in the coffin. Humans weren't the only ones being mummified; the ancient Egyptians also buried millions of animals, including mummified cats, baboons, birds, fish, and even crocodiles and hippos. Some were mummified to provide sustenance for the buried human, others to be dedicated at temples as sacred incarnations of Egyptian gods; many pets were buried alongside their owners to keep them company in the afterlife.[164]

Curious Coffins and Riveting Rituals

Mummification 101

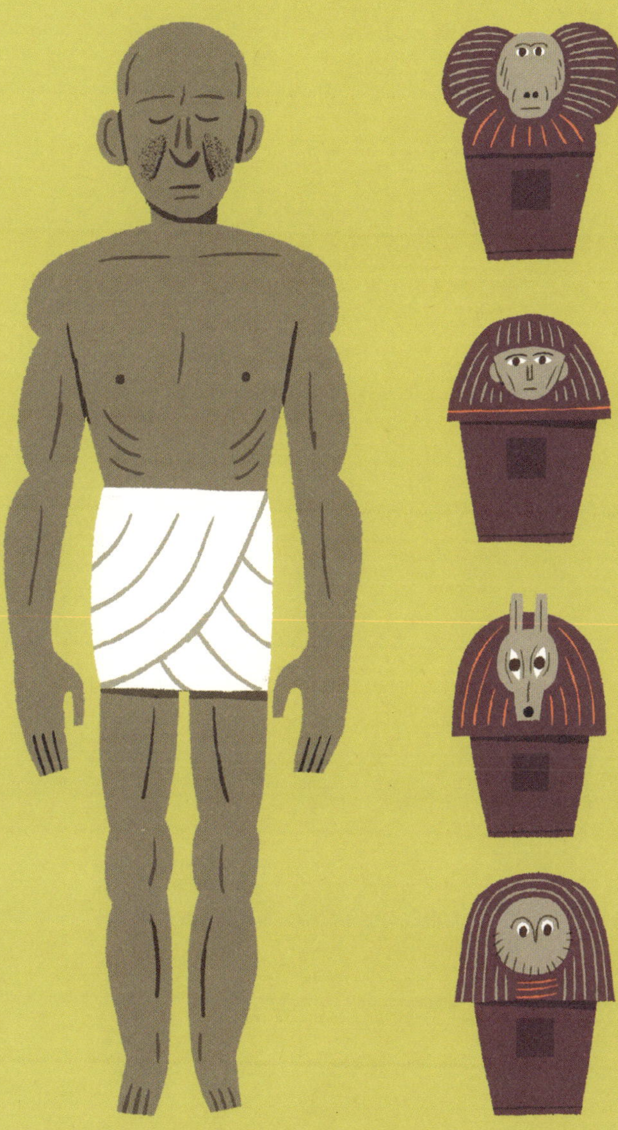

Removal of the Organs

Conducted by embalmer-priests, the Egyptian mummification process took seventy days.[165] The parts that rotted the quickest (i.e., the internal organs) were removed first. The brain was delicately scooped out with hooked tools inserted through the nostrils, while the organs in the torso were removed through an incision made on the left side of the abdomen. Only the heart, which held the ka, the essence of the deceased, was left in the body. The other organs were stored in canopic jars, which, by the time of the New Kingdom,[166] were capped with carved heads representing the four sons of the Egyptian god Horus: the baboon Hapy for the lungs, the human Imsety for the liver, the jackal Duamutef for the stomach, and the falcon Qebehsenuef for the intestines.[167] In later mummies, the organs were taken out, wrapped, and put back in place, but empty canopic jars continued to be buried with the bodies.

② Removal of Moisture

In what was probably the most tedious part of the process, the body was stuffed and covered in natron, a kind of salt gathered from the bottom of dried-up lakes, then left on a table to dry out. Once desiccated, the natron was removed and washed off.

③ Touch-Ups

Dried and hollowed-out areas of the body were reinforced with linen and other materials. False eyes were put in, and cosmetics like rouge were applied. After this, the body was washed and slathered in oils.

Curious Coffins and Riveting Rituals

④ **Wrapping of the Body**

The deceased was then wrapped in several hundred yards of linen, with resin applied between layers of fabric. Protective amulets and linen strips inscribed with magical invocations were also incorporated. Prayers were offered to prevent mishaps, and then the body was at last enshrouded in cloth and secured with linen strips.

⑤ **Encasement**

Once mummified, a death mask was affixed, and the body was encased in a coffin or sarcophagus. The number of coffins a person was buried in and the way each layer was decorated varied depending on the time period, but in general, people of influence were entombed in up to three or four wooden coffins, which were then nested in sarcophagi made of stone.

When all of this was done, the mummy was prepared for burial. For pharaohs, this entailed the preparation of a whole laundry list of grave goods ranging from food and furniture to games and statuettes. The idea was that they'd be buried with everything they could possibly need in the afterlife, which meant that artisans, servants, and court advisers were sometimes sacrificed to aid their king for eternity. Pharaohs were laid to rest in highly elaborate sarcophagi, which were then placed in great tombs, such as the Great Pyramids of Giza. While nobles and officials often received the same treatment, most people could not afford such extravagance and usually opted for simpler forms of embalming or burial. Before mummies were interred, the all-important Opening of the Mouth ceremony was conducted, during which various parts of the body were symbolically "opened" by a priest in order to awaken the senses needed to taste, hear, see, smell, and otherwise enjoy life after death.

For the Egyptians, preservation of the body was paramount to ensuring the continued survival of the spirit, which consisted of three parts: the aforementioned ka, which stayed in the tomb and used the grave goods buried with the dead; the ba, which was free to enter and leave the tomb as it pleased; and the akh, which traveled to the Duat, or afterlife, to be judged in the Weighing of the Heart, a ceremony presided over by Anubis, the god of death and mummification (whose mask would've been worn by priests throughout various stages of the mummification process). As the ceremony's name implies, the heart was weighed on a scale countered by a feather, which represented Ma'at, the goddess of order and truth. If one's soul was deemed worthy, they were admitted into the Field of Reeds—a paradise that mimicked the person's life on earth, but without discord and suffering. If the heart outweighed the feather, however, the spirit was immediately consumed by a crocodile-lion-hippopotamus entity named Ammit.[168] Also present during the judgment ceremony was Osiris, king of the underworld, whose story of death and resurrection by way of mummification forms the basis of one of ancient Egypt's most important and detailed myths.

Curious Coffins and Riveting Rituals

Mummy Mania

Fifteenth-through-nineteenth-century Europeans were obsessed with mummies. For centuries, they were traded, raided, and excavated before being shipped across the ocean. Some found their way into museum collections all across Europe, but many more went on to endure a fate far stranger. Pre-Raphaelite painters in the 1800s favored the use of "mummy brown," a rich umber shade made from a combination of white pitch, myrrh, and the ground-up remains of ancient Egyptian mummies. But it wasn't just artists who were desperate for these ground-up bodies. During the Middle Ages, powdered mummies were sold in Europe as a popular cure-all for various ailments ranging from bruising to epilepsy. Mummia, as it was then known, was typically mixed into drinks or applied externally as a salve.[169] The demand was so great that in the wake of the Egypt-wide ban on the export of mummia in the sixteenth century, a black market for fake mummies emerged. Freshly dead bodies were doctored with pitch, dried in ovens, and wrapped in linen in an attempt to fool customers. This eventually became such a big problem that leading medical authorities of the day (including Pierre Pomet, personal pharmacist to King Louis XIV) had to step in, urging shoppers to choose mummia of "a fine shining black, not full of bones and dirt, of good smell and which being burnt does not stink of pitch."[170] The misconception that mummies contained certain medicinal benefits may have come from a mistranslation of the Arabic *mūmiyā*—the term for a kind of tar used to patch up wounds—later used by Arabs to describe mummified human remains, blackened with bitumen and age, during their conquest of Egypt in the seventh century CE.[171]

Permanent Revolution

The ancient Egyptians weren't the only ones preserving their heads of state. The bodies of political leaders and nationally influential dead were sometimes embalmed and put on public display—a practice that was especially popular among dictators and Communist leaders. Flushed with pink-tinted chemicals, spotlighted by filtered lights, and kept in sterile and temperature-controlled mausoleums, these embalmed bodies served as powerful and enduring symbols of the revolution. Though many of these Communist leaders had asked not to be embalmed, their bodies were nonetheless co-opted to send a message: This political order, undefeated even by death, was not one to be trifled with.

In life, many of these figures developed a cult of personality, described by political scientist Pao-min Chang as "the artificial elevation of the status and authority of one man . . . through the deliberate creation, projection and propagation of a godlike image."[172] They often came to power during tumultuous times in their countries' histories; surrounded by political enemies and in the midst of rapid industrialization, these charismatic leaders became the nuclei of a political religion in which earthly concepts like nationhood, the state, liberty, and revolution were made sacred. Totalitarian regimes appropriated the language of faith—with its objects of worship, incorruptible bodies, and the all-encompassing power of the man at the top—to assert total control over every aspect of society, from its codes of conduct to its system of ethics.[173] Most did this deliberately to consolidate power; others, like the Russian revolutionary Vladimir Lenin, vehemently opposed public adulation in his lifetime as being antithetical to the very idea of Marxism.[174] But even he couldn't stop his body from being embalmed and venerated after his demise.

Vladimir Lenin (1870–1924)

Lenin holds the unusual honor of being the first Communist leader to be embalmed, even though he had requested to be buried with his mother. Today, he lies preserved in a giant pyramidal mausoleum on the Red Square, where he has remained for the majority of the hundred years he's been dead. Another embalmed Soviet leader, the wartime dictator Joseph Stalin, lay alongside Lenin from 1953 until his removal in 1961, when the relaxation of press censorship made it clear how unpopular he had grown with the general public.[175]

Mao Zedong (1893–1976)

Though he had asked to be cremated, the founding father of the Republic of China is as unchanging as his colossal portrait hanging over Tiananmen Square. He remains a controversial figure in China, but he retains a powerful hold on parts of the country today as a symbol of national unity,[176] and his body, forever lying in state in the Chairman Mao Memorial Hall, receives millions of visitors every year.

Ho Chi Minh (1890–1969)

The embalmed corpse of the Vietnamese revolutionary leader lies in a glass sarcophagus in his eponymous mausoleum in Hanoi, even though he too had asked to be cremated. "Uncle Ho," as he is affectionately known in Vietnam, was embalmed by the same team who had worked on Lenin's body, and Russian scientists are still regularly asked to help with the annual maintenance of the body.

The Curious Case of Eva Perón

As far as preserved heads of state went, death was pretty straightforward. You died, had your last wishes thoroughly ignored, got your body embalmed, and then were laid to rest in a glass case to be displayed for the rest of time (or at least until the tide of public opinion turned against you).

This was not how things went down for the body of first lady Eva Perón, the beloved wife of Argentine president Juan Perón. Affectionately known as Evita, she was born into poverty before finding fame as a radio and film actor. Her philanthropic efforts and humble beginnings made her massively popular with Argentina's working class, whom she called descamisados, or "shirtless ones"—a derogatory term used by Argentine elites to mock Perón's supporters that was later reclaimed as a powerful rallying cry. Her untimely death from cancer at age thirty-three on July 26, 1952, spurred a public outpouring of grief so intense that the country all but screeched to a halt for ten days.

Unbeknownst to Eva, her husband had arranged for renowned physician Pedro Ara to begin embalming her the minute she died. And so he did; over the course of the next few years, all her blood was replaced with glycerin to preserve her organs, and her skin was coated in a thin layer of plastic. Her husband had intended to display her body in a monument larger than the Statue of Liberty, no doubt because she had inspired a level of public affection you did *not* simply leave to waste as a politician.[177] Unfortunately for Juan Perón, that never came to pass, as he was overthrown in a military coup in 1955. Eva's body was confiscated for fear that it would be used to spark a rebellion, and it spent the next two years in various nooks and crannies across the country, including inside a parked van, hidden behind a cinema screen, and tucked away in the offices of the men who had abducted her. With the help of the Vatican, her body was taken to Italy to be buried in Milan under a false name.

But the people of Argentina did not forget their Evita. Graffiti all around the city demanded to know where she was, and in 1970, General Pedro Eugenio Aramburu was assassinated by Peronist guerillas. Eva's body—now slightly battered and a finger short—was eventually delivered to the exiled Juan Perón, who was by then living in Spain with his third wife, Isabel. Eva made her way home after Juan's reelection as president in 1973. Upon his death just a year later, Isabel Perón took over as president of Argentina and began making plans to inter Eva's body in yet another monument. Shockingly, in 1976, she was spared this fate yet again when Isabel's government was overthrown in Argentina's bloodiest coup yet. Eva's body was finally returned to her family's mausoleum in Buenos Aires, where she lies buried in what is essentially a giant metal bunker.[178]

Today, Juan Perón's (and by extension, Eva's) legacy remains controversial. The pair enjoyed widespread support from the Argentine working class—when the country's economy wasn't in the gutter, that is—with Juan elected president thrice.[179] Eva, in particular, was a stalwart proponent of women's suffrage and remains a powerful symbol among the poor and oppressed.[180] On the flip side, Juan also infamously idolized Mussolini, and his terms in office were punctuated by bouts of violence and marked by suspiciously fascist activities, such as the restriction of the nation's press and the jailing of political opponents. But regardless of how you view the Peróns, one thing is clear: From the moment Evita died, she ceased being her own person. Her strange twenty-year-long posthumous odyssey is a testament to the cycle of dehumanization that political figures occasionally undergo after a lifetime of turning man into myth.

THE HUSBAND
JUAN PERÓN
THE EMBALMER
PEDRO ARA
THE USURPER
GEN. PEDRO E. ARAMBURU
THE THIRD WIFE
ISABEL PERÓN

Sleep Tight

Artificially preserving a body was, for most of history, accessible to only the rich and powerful. But if you were to journey to the Capuchin Catacombs of Palermo, Italy, you'd be met with the preserved bodies of 1,284 people from all walks of life.

The catacombs functioned as a cemetery for the Convent of the Capuchin Friars until a group of forty-five monks were found miraculously preserved. The Capuchins decided against reburying them, believing the discovery to be a divine act of providence. They instead displayed their brothers as relics by placing them in niches along the walls of the catacombs. Most of the bodies were mummified by dehydrating the corpses in a colatoio—a kind of dry room that stripped the dead of all bodily fluids. After about a year, the desiccated corpses were washed in vinegar and redressed.[181] Though only monks were mummified at first, the brothers eventually began preserving and displaying the corpses of the local dead.

The catacombs have enthralled writers and artists for centuries, with eighteenth-century Italian poet Ippolito Pindemonte writing that for the bodies displayed in Palermo, "death . . . seems to have missed all shots."[182] Grouped according to age, sex, occupation, and social status, mummies at various stages of decay are displayed in open coffins, piled onto shelves, and hung from the walls of the narrow corridors. Some are hundreds of years old, with the oldest being that of Friar Silvestro da Gubbio, who died in 1599.[183] Time has sadly ravaged many of the mummies; some are missing noses, others their cheeks and eyes. Gravity and the gradual loosening of facial ligaments have contorted many of their faces in a way that makes them look like they are in the midst of a never-ending scream.[184]

The Master of Eternal Slumber

In the Capuchin Catacombs of Palermo, only a few bodies have been chemically embalmed, including the rosy-faced Antonio Prestigiacomo, who was preserved in arsenic—a common practice during epidemics.[185] However, the most famous embalmed body is, without a doubt, that of Rosalia Lombardo, an Italian toddler who died of pneumonia in 1918. She was embalmed by a Sicilian chemist named Alfredo Salafia at the request of her heartbroken father, and she was one of the last corpses to be admitted into the catacombs. Thousands of tourists flock to see her every year, and indeed, as she appears to have merely fallen asleep beneath her glass display case over a hundred years after her death, there's little wonder why. She is so well-preserved that according to Sicilian legend, if you stay in the catacombs long enough, you will see her eyes slowly open.

Curious Coffins and Riveting Rituals

✝
FRATE
SILVESTRO DA
GUBBIO
OCT 1599

The Living Dead

In Tana Toraja, Indonesia, death is seen as a gradual social process, and one is only considered dead once a funeral deemed worthy of their status in life has been held. These funerals are a big deal, often drawing crowds in the hundreds. They're also expensive, so it can take families a long time to accumulate the funds necessary to afford one. In the interim, life goes on in the presence of the dead: The bodies of family members are embalmed, kept within the household, and generally treated as though they are still alive until a suitable funeral can be held. They are referred to as being merely sick or asleep and are symbolically fed, dressed, and cared for—sometimes for years after they've died.

Indonesia may be majority Muslim, but in South Sulawesi, the Toraja traditionally adhered to an animistic religion known as Aluk to Dolo—roughly translating to "the beliefs of the people bygone"—which flourished up until Christianity was introduced under Dutch rule in the early 1900s.[186] Their death rituals, however, have survived. In the past, bodies were mummified using chemicals similar to those employed by taxidermists looking to stiffen and strengthen animal hide: various oils, tea leaves, and tree bark.[187] Today, they're preserved with formalin and other modern embalming fluids. Food is brought to the corpses daily, along with tea and other offerings. Death is not kept away from the living, not even from the youngest members of the family. In fact, many children recall sleeping in the same bed as their dead grandparents for years on end.[188]

When it finally comes time for the funeral, guests form a large procession and offer up gifts of sacrificial animals, as well as food and drink. Accompanied by the beating of drums and the clashing of cymbals, the deceased is transferred into a scaled-down replica of a tongkonan—a traditional Torajan dwelling. The house, hoisted atop the shoulders of the funerary procession, has a distinct boat-shaped roof that swoops upward, angled to aid in the soul's transmigration to Puya, the afterlife.[189]

Central to Torajan funerary rites is the killing of sacrificial
animals such as buffalo and pigs, and it is only after the death
of the first animal that the "illness" that befell the human body
is said to have ended. In Tana Toraja, funerals vary greatly
depending on social status. For someone of great importance, it
is common practice to sacrifice hundreds of buffalo as a sign of
respect and love for the deceased.[190] Buffalo are seen as guides
and escorts for the spirits of the dead, whom they carry on
their backs into the afterlife and whom they keep from hanging
around and bringing misfortune upon the living. When all is
done, the meat from the slain animals is distributed to guests,
with those of stature bringing home the best cuts.[191]

A week later, the village brings the coffin to its final resting
place, which is typically a vault on a cliff face. Sometimes,
wooden ancestral effigies known as tau tau are left to guard
the casket.[192] Every few years, families return to their ancestral
tombs for a "second funeral" called ma'nene, where the bodies
of the dead are taken out of their coffins to be dressed in new
sets of clothes. For the Torajan people, none of this is unusual
or scary. When a Torajan man was asked by author and
photographer Paul Koudounaris if he had understood why
the cadaver of his grandfather was treated this way as a
child, the man simply replied, "Because we loved him."[193]

Deadly Diet

For the most dedicated Buddhist monks, the preservation process began before death. Since the eleventh century in Japan, people known as "living Buddhas" underwent a ritual of self-mummification called sokushinbutsu, or "becoming a Buddha in this very body."[194]

Many of the self-made mummies belonged to the mountain-dwelling followers of Shugendō, a syncretic form of Shintoism and esoteric Buddhism that stresses suffering and self-sacrifice. These monks were no strangers to ascetic rituals, such as meditating in caves, partaking in cold-water ablutions, and starving themselves for extended periods of time. The idea was that these acts of endurance and suffering would bring a profane man closer to the divine, which is why if you venture deep into the mountains of Yamagata, there's a chance that you may encounter a number of mummies still clad in their priestly robes and prayer beads, caught in a perpetual state of meditation. Some of the mummies are remarkably well-preserved despite being more than three hundred years old.[195]

But immortality did not come easily. Self-mummification took about ten years to complete, throughout which the monk maintained a strict and excruciating diet called mokujikigyō, or, literally, "tree eating."[196] This meant subsisting on a diet of berries, nuts, and seeds, as well as food-adjacent things like tree bark and pine needles, all while embarking on a high-intensity physical regimen that stripped them of as much body fat as possible (which is important because fat accelerates the decomposition process due to its high water content).[197] They abstained from drinking any liquids aside from a tea made with the toxic sap of the urushi tree—an ingredient much more commonly used to lacquer wood. The vomiting that inevitably ensued desiccated the body, while the poisonous tea sap ensured that the body would not be consumed by decomposers. This diet was gradually winnowed even further over the following decade, resulting in what was essentially a drawn-out death by starvation.

Once he knew that death was upon him, the monk would then bury himself alive in a chamber supplied with nothing but a bamboo air tube and a bell, which he was expected to ring daily. The tomb was sealed on the day the bell fell silent, and it was only opened three years later to make sure that the monk had indeed been mummified.[198] Those who made it were enshrined, while those who didn't (which is to say, most of them) were exorcised and reburied.[199] The practice has since been outlawed, but like their Catholic counterparts, the incorruptible bodies of these bodhisattvas are still seen as holy. They sit enshrined in temples all over northern Japan, where they are ceremonially disrobed and redressed once every six years. The discarded robes are turned into purchasable protective amulets.

The Coolest Mummy in the World

Buddhist bodhisattvas continue to be revered
across countries such as Thailand, China, and India.
The body of Luang Pho Daeng, a seventy-nine-
year-old Buddhist monk who died while meditating in 1973, is currently on display at the Thai
temple of Wat Khunaram. In the final seven days
leading up to his death, he stopped eating and
drinking—a sign that he had reached the highest
form of enlightenment through the rejection of all
worldly desires. As with the mummified monks of
Yamagata, this ritual dehydrated his body, which
in turn resulted in a naturally mummified corpse.
Today, he sits peacefully inside a glass case on the
paradisiacal island of Ko Samui, clad in a pair of
sunglasses that hide his sunken eye sockets.[200]

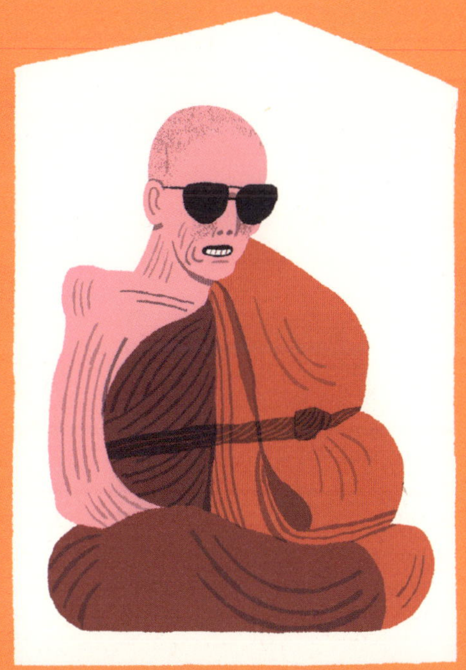

The American Way of Death

When someone dies in the United States, embalming is often treated as a matter of course, regardless of your chosen method of disposition. In fact, it's one of the few countries in the world where embalming the dead is common practice.[201] In *The American Way of Death*, a landmark book published in 1963, Jessica Mitford offers a scathing critique of the predatory industrial forces that run the modern funeral complex in the United States. In it, morticians are skewered for offering up deceitful claims that embalming is more traditional, more hygienic, and necessary.[202] But the embalming craze in the United States didn't just come out of nowhere. To understand how it managed to gain such a foothold in the country, we must travel back to the American Civil War.

Up until that point, most Americans died in the comfort of their own homes, where they were allowed to make their peace with God while surrounded by family. Within forty-eight hours, the body would be washed, redressed, displayed for viewing, and delivered to the graveyard for the final disposition. The Civil War made this practically impossible, and the American art of dying was never the same again. By the end of 1865, the war had claimed the lives of more than six hundred thousand people, making it the single bloodiest war in American history. Many soldiers died far from home, hastily buried without ceremony and dumped into unmarked graves.[203]

This all changed in 1861, when Colonel Elmer Ellsworth—generally considered to be the first known Union casualty of the war—was shot and killed during his attempt to remove a Confederate flag from the roof of a hotel in Virginia. The media pounced on every detail of his death, including the strikingly lifelike appearance of his corpse lying in state. His body had been embalmed by Thomas Holmes, the man who would come to be known as the father of American embalming.[204] At the time, the practice of embalming had been restricted to preserving cadavers in medical schools, but as families grew increasingly concerned about the whereabouts of their slaughtered kin (as well as the questionable states of their troubled souls), people began finding new ways to send the bodies home. Unfortunately, airtight coffins and icy caskets could only do so much to forestall decomposition on those long train rides, so the demand for embalmers grew.[205]

A host of freelance embalmers answered the call, to varying degrees of professionalism and success—some embalmed the dead without consent, while others made it their business to scope out battlefields *as* the battles were being fought.[206] Abraham Lincoln himself was embalmed following his assassination, and as he lay in state, thousands bore witness to an embalming job well done: It was as if he had never been shot, as if he were simply sleeping.[207] For the grieving American public, the preservation of bodies—once the purview of God and his saints—had at last moved into the realm of industry and science.

Hostilities eventually came to an end, leaving a booming industry of fully fledged embalmers scrambling. In the years following, undertakers continued to peddle the idea that everyone should be embalmed after they died, citing a need to keep them around long enough to allow long-distance mourners a chance to pay their last respects. Today, the practice is ubiquitous across the United States, although it is not without its detractors.

Save It for Later
How Bodies Are Embalmed

① Enter: the Body

After someone dies, their body is collected and wheeled into the funeral home on a gurney, usually through an entrance separate from the one used by grieving loved ones. All the embalming takes place in a well-ventilated preparation room, which is outfitted as such so that the toxic fumes released during the process have somewhere to go.

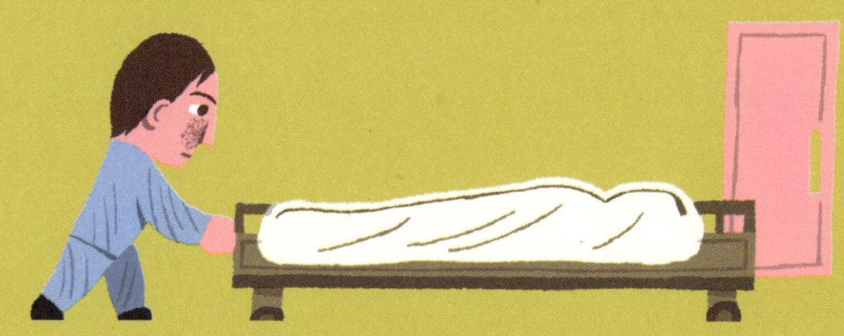

② Initial Evaluation

The mortician (dressed in full protective gear to limit exposure to blood, pathogens, and embalming fluids, many of which contain toxic aldehydes) looks over the body and takes stock of what needs to be done. Their main goals are as follows: (1) sanitization, (2) preservation, and (3) restoration, which can entail anything from masking decomposition to reconstructing injured body parts.

③ Setting the Features

After the various cavities of the face, such as the nose and ears, have been cleaned with a cotton swab, eye caps are inserted behind the eyelids to mask the sunken eyeballs underneath and to prevent an unwelcome reopening of the eyes at the funeral. The mouth is sometimes shaped with a mouth former before the mortician comes in with a needle injector to punch wires through the upper and lower jaw and seal it shut.

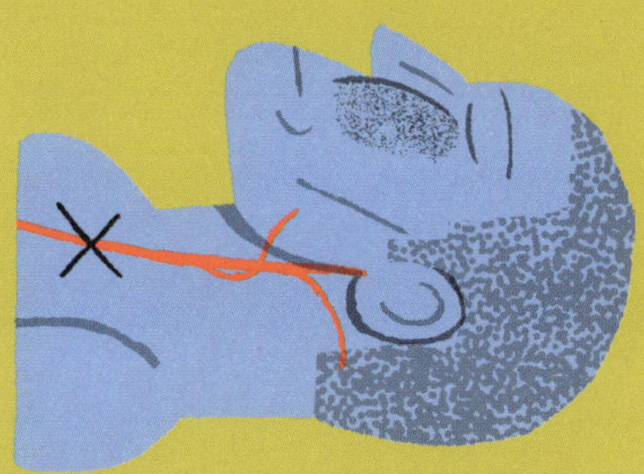

❹ Arterial Embalming

Next, an embalming machine is used to pump the body full of preservative chemicals. But before that can be done, the mortician must find an artery. The most commonly used entry point is the carotid artery in the neck, though the large femoral artery in the leg is a good alternative. Occasionally, the mortician might have to dig around a little to find either artery, using tools with delightful names such as tissue spreader, aneurysm hook, and drain tube. A small metal tube is inserted into the chosen artery, and in goes a cocktail of formaldehyde and alcohol—some of which helps forestall decomposition, while the rest helps replenish volume and rosiness.[208]

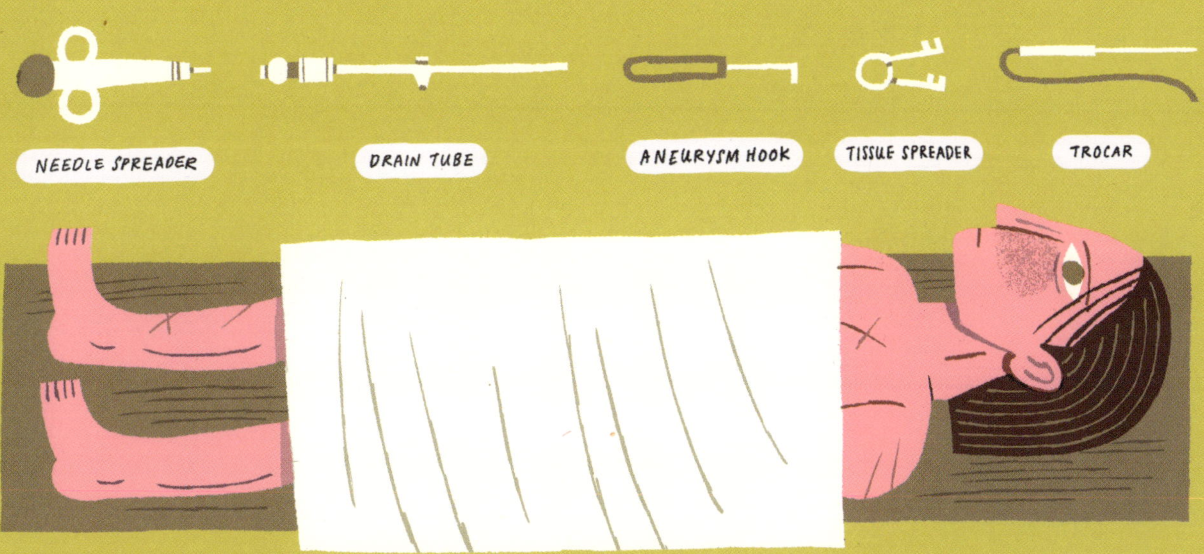

❺ Cavity Embalming

A long, stabby instrument known as a trocar is then used to puncture the organs, vacuuming up the gas and liquids within and replacing them with cavity fluid, which restores lost volume and kills the mass of bacteria hiding within.

❻ Final Touches

Makeup is applied (along with various pastes, plasters, and wax, depending on the extent of the decomposition or injury), the hair is arranged, and the corpse is changed into its final set of clothes, which may or may not be provided by the deceased's family. After that, the body is at last placed into the casket and delivered to the funeral or grave site.

Very Dead

HOW DO WE REMEMBER OUR DEAD?

"Someday soon, perhaps in forty years, there will be no one alive who has ever known me. . . . Whose death will make me truly dead?"[1] —IRVIN D. YALOM

PART I

Rituals of Remembrance

Good Grief

While some cultures call for the complete destruction of anything that might remind the living of the deceased (such as the aforementioned Wari' people, for whom it is customary to obliterate by fire everything associated with someone who has died), just *getting over it* is a lot easier said than done. You don't just stop thinking about your uncle Jim the moment his body is laid to rest under four feet of dirt or packed neatly into a nice ceramic urn; love tends to linger, and as a consequence, so does grief.

Many of our death rituals go on long after the final disposition of our dead, and no discussion about the culture of death is complete without talking about the ways we mourn and commemorate our dearly departed.

Almost every culture that has ever existed has ritualized mourning in some way, giving all of us an outlet through which we may express our grief and (hopefully) attain some measure of catharsis and

closure. These rituals can take place days, weeks, and even years after someone has died, and they often entail some degree of repetition. They can call for the participation of any number of people, from private ceremonies to state funerals and holidays involving entire regions and countries. Through private acts of remembrance, special ceremonies, and festivals of death, the dead live on through the memories of the living.

So why do so many of us feel compelled to revisit our dead, often repeatedly, years after the fact? Many of these rituals are, ostensibly, acts of compassion for our dead. We offer them food, leave them their favorite toys and flowers and cigarettes, and occasionally exhume and clothe their corpses—all to ensure a cushy afterlife, wherever they are. Sometimes we do this out of fear of retribution, believing that failing to perform certain rituals will invoke the wrath of our ancestors or gods. Other times, these gestures serve as an extension of daily life from when the dead were still, well, *alive*, thus making the sudden transition from presence to absence considerably less jarring. For example, in cultures that actively worship or venerate their ancestors, the line that separates ritual life from "normal" life can be nearly imperceptible. Death is made part of life, and little by little, the stability, structure, and predictability of tradition help us navigate the treacherous and disorienting waters of grief. With festivals and holidays geared toward the commemoration of the dead, both known and unknown, entire communities are drawn together to share in the act of collective remembrance— something that unites us in a common identity and connects us to some higher purpose. And these festivals aren't always particularly somber either, making it clear that rituals of remembrance are there not only to help us make sense of death but also to serve as a celebration of life.

Perhaps the most important function of commemorative rituals is this: We do for others what we want others to do for us. There will come a day when we'll exist only in the memories of those who survive us, and these ceremonies give us a taste of what we're in for after we reach our own inevitable ends. In other words, we keep our dead alive because, like it or not, we'll be in their company soon enough.

Theater of Sorrow

In most cultures, death is marked by some kind of ceremony wherein the deceased is visited and bade farewell one final time. More often than not, this takes the form of a funeral or memorial service, which usually precedes or happens concurrently with the body's final interment, regardless of the method of disposition.

Though the way we personally express our sadness may feel instinctive, the way we mourn, particularly at public or semipublic events, is often dictated by the many cultural norms with which we were raised. These oft-unspoken social rules govern how we're expected to dress and conduct ourselves, and funerals can feel very different from culture to culture. For example, a Nigerian attending an elderly person's funeral in the United States for the first time might find the generally somber atmosphere discomfiting; in Nigeria, the death of an elder is seen as the conclusion of a life fully lived, and as such, the funeral is lighthearted and celebratory. On the other hand, funerals for dead children are considered so unbearable in their wrongness that parents are almost always absent from them.[2] Depending on where you are, loud, uncontrollable wailing at a funeral may be expected in one community but abhorred in another. Historically (and in pockets of the world today), professional mourners were hired to perform grief in places like Greece, Egypt, China, and India, where they trailed after the dead, eulogizing, wailing, tearing at their hair, and beating their breasts. Likewise, holding a funeral that is lavish or well planned can be seen as a performative ritual; in Chinese culture, it is considered par for the course to provide your parents with a funeral that outwardly displays pride, respect, and filial care for the deceased.[3]

Formal funerary ceremonies may have stricter expectations in place with regard to expected dress and decorum, and there are perhaps no funeral rites more laden with ceremony than those held

Curious Coffins and Riveting Rituals

by the state.[4] Public and state funerals, particularly those reserved for presidents and monarchs, are often colossal undertakings spanning several days. Ceremonies are often held across multiple locations. In the United States, presidential state funerals have thus far been conducted within the states in which the presidents lived; in Washington, DC, where the presidents worked; and, lastly, in the states where the presidents agreed to be interred.[5] They have also been marked by widely attended events, such as the processions conveying the presidents' bodies to the sites where they lay in state, hearkening back to the spectacle of saintly reliquaries paraded through the streets to the churches where they were going to be enshrined. Winston Churchill's coffin received more than 321,000 visitors, and 350 million more watched the funeral proceedings on television.[6]

State funerals in the United States are typically reserved for key figures in the federal government, distinguished civilians of national import, and presidents past and present. The national flag features prominently in several proceedings: The Stars and Stripes is flown at half-mast, denoting a period of national mourning. One is also draped over the coffins of presidents and military personnel—which,

along with the 21-gun salute, make up just some of the military honors bestowed upon the esteemed dead. The funeral of President John F. Kennedy has been described as a "ritualized occasion of the greatest social necessity," in the sense that the sudden and violent assassination of a figure thought to represent an entire nation required an equally dramatic ritual to reunite a fragmented country. The funeral took place over four days, and Joseph Campbell described the experience as "the first and only thing of its kind in peacetime that has ever given me the sense of being a member of this whole national community, engaged as a unit in the observance of a deeply significant rite."[7]

Dress to Depress

Whether the recently bereaved were attending a funeral or entering a period of mourning, grief was historically expressed through clothing. As with all ritual events marking some kind of social change, death was acknowledged as a significant event through the outward display of sorrow and solemnity. Many cultures ascribed symbolic meaning to certain colors and articles of clothing, and mourning outfits were often clearly distinct from those worn in daily life. Mourning attire served a dual function: It was a gesture of respect for the dead, and it signaled to others that the bereaved had recently suffered a loss. In certain cultures, this might have meant that the mourner was entering a period of social seclusion.[8]

Typically, the kind of clothes one wore—along with how long they were expected to wear them—was dictated by certain rules of etiquette specific to each culture. The rules often varied according to a person's gender, relation to the deceased, and social class. In recent times, mourning has become a lot less prescriptive. As the world has grown increasingly interconnected, Western-style suits and black clothing have gradually become the norm across many different countries, including those where white, not black, has commonly been the traditional color of mourning.

Australia

Gypsum mourning caps known as kopis were traditionally worn for up to six months by Aboriginal Australians mourning the death of an important clan member or loved one. The bereaved shaved their heads and applied a layer of netting over their scalps, after which the cap was applied onto the head layer by layer. The greater the number of layers, the stronger the grief. When completed, a kopi could be one to two inches thick and weigh anywhere between four and seventeen pounds. They were almost always white—the color for mourning in most Indigenous Australian cultures. When it came time to move on, the kopis were taken off and left on the graves of the deceased.[9]

England

By the Middle Ages, much of Europe had already begun associating the color black with death due to its being perceived as both sophisticated and somber. This was affirmed and concretized during the Victorian era—a period known for its rigid social codes for mourning, popularized by its eponymous queen. These rules dictated everything from the expected length of mourning periods (a year and a day for a widow mourning a husband, and six to twelve months for a child mourning a parent) to the kinds of dresses women were allowed to wear (black dresses, veils, gloves, shoes, and simple untrimmed bonnets when in deep mourning; lilacs, purples, and grays upon entering light mourning).[10]

Ghana

Ghanaian funerals are weeklong affairs attended by hundreds, and they can cost almost as much as weddings; attending one underdressed is therefore considered incredibly inappropriate. Red is traditionally worn by close relatives of the deceased. Other mourners, including distant family members, typically wear black. If the deceased died of old age, white is worn to celebrate a life well lived.[11]

Korea

In cultures influenced by Confucianism, such as Korean culture, traditional mourning attire usually differed according to one's kinship with the deceased. During the Joseon dynasty (1392–1910) mourners donned five different forms of funerary clothing called obok. They were classified by the quality of hemp from which they were made, with the roughest reserved for the chief mourner.[12] Close relatives were expected to wear obok for three months to three years. Today, funerals in Korea last three days, and white obok have mostly been phased out in favor of black sangbok—a different type of mourning wear consisting of a suit for men and a hanbok (traditional dress) for women.

A Grave Affair

A common ritual practiced across the world is the continual revisiting of graves, particularly on special occasions such as days of national commemoration or birthdays and anniversaries. Visitors often find it meaningful to mark each visit with grave offerings, which are often objects that possess special symbolic meaning.

Candles

Candles feature in the mourning rites of countless people, from the ancient Romans to present-day Hindus—another testament to the ritual significance and cross-cultural sanctity of fire. In Christianity, a burning candle is associated with God's holy presence as the Father of Light, while the ancient Macedonians lit candles to deter ghosts and other evil forces from coming after the souls of the deceased. For some, a lit candle declares to others that the memory of the departed still burns bright, while others may see a flickering flame as symbolic of the fleeting nature of our time on earth.

Alcohol (and Other Liquids)

A libation—from the Latin *libatio*—refers to the ritual pouring of drink. Although it appears in various cultures, it is once again most closely associated with the ancient Greeks, who liberally libated at events ranging from ritual sacrifices to banquets and business meetings. The liquids spilled were typically water, wine, milk, oil, or honey. The original symbolic function is ambiguous, but libations came to be understood as acts of purification for the living, and as nourishment for the dead.[13]

Visiting Stones

This ancient Jewish custom may not be enshrined in any law or scripture, but the ritual of leaving stones on tombs and graves has been practiced for centuries. Explanations vary, but some think it might've stemmed from the days of nomadic life, when many Jews were interred in shallow graves across arid regions and rocks were used to weigh the bodies down. The dead were also covered with stones during the First Temple period (1200 to 586 BCE) to warn Jewish priests to keep their distance, lest they become ritually impure by coming within four feet of a dead body.[14] In any case, stones are seen as markers of eternal remembrance because, unlike flowers, they don't rot.

"I Voted" Stickers

Voting stickers have appeared on the gravestone of beloved suffragette Susan B. Anthony every election cycle since 2014, more than a century after her death. Though the gravestone currently sports a plastic sleeve for fear of adhesive-induced damage, it remains an important pilgrimage site for many women eager to celebrate her legacy.[15] It's one of the many famous graves honored with grave goods that reference the legacies left by their eminent occupants. Other such instances include the many ballet shoes dedicated to Sergei Diaghilev, founder of the Ballets Russes, and Roald Dahl's grave, on which peaches and chocolates periodically appear.

Coins

The practice of leaving coins with the dead is most closely associated with the ancient Greek belief that the dead require a token to get across the river Styx. In more recent times, leaving coins on the graves of American soldiers became popular during the Vietnam War, since it was seen as a subtle yet powerful way to commemorate the dead without inciting a political discussion about the ethicality of the war itself. There was even a language to it: Leaving a penny meant that you had simply dropped by to pay respects; a nickel indicated that you had trained with the deceased, a dime that you served alongside them, and a quarter that you had witnessed their death.[16]

Red Poppies
White Chrysanthemums
White Lilies

Pushing Up Daisies

The Language of Flowers

The most common grave offering of them all is, perhaps, flowers, which have held immense cross-cultural significance for millennia. All of life's milestones (births, first loves, bouts of illness) are frequently tied to the gift of flowers—delicate, beautiful, and ephemeral, each symbolic of something different. Death, of course, is no exception.

Red Poppies: Popularized by John McCrae's wartime poem "In Flanders Fields," red poppies flourished on the battlefields of World War I and are frequently worn across the United States, Britain, and the Commonwealth nations on Remembrance Day (or Veterans Day, if you're from the United States) to commemorate those who died in the line of duty.[17]

White Chrysanthemums: Associated with purity, longevity, and bereavement, white chrysanthemums are popular funeral flowers throughout parts of Europe and Asia (particularly China, Japan, and Korea).[18]

White Lilies: These fragrant flowers are an early Christian symbol of purity and virtue, and it is said that the grave of the Virgin Mary was covered in them following her assumption into heaven.[19]

Violets: Owing to their short lifespans, violets were used to honor the dead in ancient Greece and Rome and are a recurring motif in Shakespeare's plays as symbols of untimely death.[20]

Marigolds: Beloved for their strong fragrance and vibrancy, marigolds are a common sight on ofrendas during the Mexican Day of the Dead, when they are used to lead the spirits of the departed back home.[21] Ever since Spanish and Portuguese traders brought them to India some 350 years ago, they have also become a common sight at Indian cremation sites and festive occasions like weddings.[22]

Forget Me Not

Victorian England was obsessed with death. The years between 1837 and 1901 were rife with tragedy and disease. Epidemics like typhus, cholera, and diphtheria ran rampant throughout the country, infant mortality rates soared, and mourning wasn't just constant—it was in vogue. This was a period that saw its eponymous queen, Victoria, plunged into grief over the death of her husband, Prince Albert, in 1861, leaving her in a state of perpetual mourning; she wore black every day for the next forty years, until the day she died. Mourning was strictly organized and controlled, and manuals detailing the kinds of clothes people had to wear and how long they were expected to mourn were extremely popular among Victorian housewives. Other rituals allowed for more private expressions of grief, and it was common for family members to keep locks of hair from the dead in small jars, lockets, and other kinds of jewelry as mementos.

The popularity of hairwork jewelry, prized for its resistance to decay and its obvious association with the person to whom it belonged, skyrocketed in the mid-nineteenth century. Some pieces incorporated hair belonging to multiple people across several generations and were meant to be passed down as treasured heirlooms, while others were traded as thoughtful gifts between friends and lovers.[23] The idea that locks of hair could serve as stand-ins for certain people may have its roots in the saintly reliquaries of the Middle Ages.[24] Like those sacred receptacles, these tokens of remembrance allowed for private communion between the wearer and the enshrined. There is also something deeply comforting about the immutability of hair; skin loses its color, and flesh bloats and rots away, but locks of hair remain unchanging.

The practice of imbuing someone's hair with death-defying or commemorative power is shared with other cultures as well. Common to many Native American tribes is the belief that the soul resides in one's hair; the Lakota dead traditionally have a lock of hair removed, purified, and wrapped in buckskin to form what is known as a "soul bundle." This is kept indoors for a period of ritualized mourning that usually lasts a year or so before it is brought outside, upon which the soul is ritually released.[25] Hair occupies such a sacred spot in many Native American societies that some today still refuse to cut the hair of their children for fear of disrupting the developing soul.[26]

Still Life

Victorian England was also home to another tradition: postmortem photography. As photography became cheaper and more accessible, more and more families jumped at the chance to obtain what was perhaps the most powerful keepsake of all: a snapshot of a loved one taken before death and decay stole them away forever.

A lot of effort went into making the photos lifelike; corpses were photographed with living family members, and children were sometimes posed as if asleep. Some subjects were photographed with flowers or their favorite dolls, toys, and stuffed animals. To further the illusion, cheeks and lips were sometimes tinted, and eyes were painted onto closed eyelids . . . with varying degrees of success.

Dancing with the Dead

In Madagascar, the ancestral tombs of the Malagasy dead are cracked open and exhumed every five to seven years during a ritual known as famadihana (pronounced "fa-ma-DEE-an"), or "the turning of the bones." Like many other communities, the Malagasy believe that the dead hold incredible power as intermediaries between God and the living.

According to historian Andrianahaga Mahery, the process starts when an ancestor appears to a senior family member in a dream, telling them that they are cold and need new clothes. Astrological sages known as ombiasy are then consulted to determine the best day to open and close the tomb.[27] During the celebrations, people near and far journey to these family crypts to unearth the decomposing bodies of their dead, who are doused in wine or perfume before being redressed in fresh silk shrouds known as lamba, which are woven rectangular shawls worn by both the living and the dead. And it is celebratory—the families dance with the bones of the deceased as a band plays live music. For some, it's a chance to update their deceased relatives with family news and ask for blessings; for others, it's a chance to remember and tell stories about the dead. Either way, it is understood to be a joyous occasion, so people dance, chat, and get drunk, and few tears are shed. The ritual ends just before sundown, at which time the bodies are reinterred headfirst alongside gifts of alcohol and food, signaling that they have once again entered the world of the ancestral dead.[28]

The spirits of the Malagasy are believed to periodically pass between the worlds of the living and the dead until their bodies have decomposed entirely.[29] Famadihana is a continuation of a long tradition of ancestral worship, and relatives will often participate in the ritual regardless of their religious affiliation. Many are willing to pay huge sums of money to construct a crypt, which, in addition to being the spiritual focus of rituals such as these, also signals to others that a family has considerable prosperity and prestige. For them, famadihana is necessary to maintain ties with one's familial past and to pay tribute to one's ancestors, to whom the living owe everything.

Spring Cleaning

There are few cultures more closely associated with the veneration of the ancestral dead than the Chinese, both in China and its international diaspora. The Qingming Festival, also known as Tomb Sweeping Day, takes place fifteen days after the spring equinox according to the lunar calendar, which is usually in early April. As its name suggests, it is a day for people to clean the tombs of their familial dead. For those interred in the ground, weeds around the tomb are removed and the dirt surrounding the grave is refreshed before offerings are made to the dead. Today, many of these "tombs" are located in columbariums, which are also cleaned.

Tomb Sweeping Day is a national holiday in China and other parts of Asia, where it is widely observed.

It is primarily seen as an expression of filial piety, the Confucian virtue of having respect for one's elders, especially one's parents, grandparents, and ancestors. Historically, it was a time for people from all social strata to pay respects to those who came before them—not only as a show of gratitude but also for fear of spiritual retribution from disgruntled ancestors.

After the tomb is cleaned, family members typically leave their forebears offerings of incense, food, and wine. Many families burn joss paper—sheets of bamboo or rice paper that serve as stand-ins for money, clothing, personal electronics, household goods, and other things deemed necessary in the afterlife. The offerings are then conveyed into the spirit world through the fire's smoke.[30]

Hungry Ghosts

A related but distinct festival is held on the fifteenth day of the seventh lunar month—the month of ghosts, which usually falls sometime between August and early September. On Zhong Yuan Jie, also known as the Hungry Ghost Festival (observed in Taiwan, parts of mainland China, and among the Chinese diaspora of Southeast Asia), the gates of the underworld are opened, and its spectral occupants are released into the world of the living. These ghosts are believed to wander the earth in search of food and entertainment. As during Tomb Sweeping Day, people leave offerings of food and incense on altars set up along the streets. Paper money and other paper effigies representing various luxuries and necessities are burned on open fires or inside special containers and pits located in temples, clearings, or the streets. Large-scale burnings are often witnessed by a large paper effigy of Da Shi Ye, the King of Hell. He is, in actuality, Guan Yin, the goddess of mercy, who takes on this fearsome form in order to intimidate and control restless spirits.[31] Throughout the month, Taoist priests perform rites to appease the dead, and unlike during the Qingming Festival, all the dead—regardless of age or relation—are honored and provided for.

But, this reverential treatment of the dead is also tinged with fear, and superstitions abound. It's considered an inauspicious time for marrying, making large purchases, or moving out, and special care is taken to avoid incurring the wrath of the dead by stepping on or kicking offerings left at street altars. Fearful of running into or attracting evil spirits, many refrain from wearing red or going out after dark, and others make it a point to steer clear of excessive drinking, as it's thought to be easier for ghosts to possess the intoxicated.[32]

Day of the Dead

Día de los Muertos, otherwise known as the Day of the Dead, is celebrated on the first and second days of November in Mexico. Festivities can start as early as October 28, with each day corresponding to a different group of people, from unbaptized children to those who died in accidents.[33] During this time, the boundary separating the worlds of the living and the dead is thought to disappear completely, allowing the spirits of the deceased to return home. The mood is anything but dour; during Día de los Muertos, death is celebrated. Homes, storefronts, and cemeteries are awash in explosions of color, light, and music; skulls and skeletons adorn every surface, appearing on puppets, candy, and little loaves of bread known as pan de muerto. Calaveras literarias, or "literary skulls"—short and often amusing satiric verses describing the living as if they were dead—are exchanged between family, friends, and colleagues.[34] The air hangs heavy with the smell of freshly cut marigolds and copal, a precolonial incense, as families gather to honor and welcome their departed loved ones.

Preparations start early; weeks in advance, flowers are sown, materials for ofrendas are gathered, and homes are swept and decorated. On the first day, tombs are swept and offerings laid out. The dead are commemorated with ofrendas, which, on Día de los Angelitos (Day of the Little Angels), are typically filled with the favorite snacks, candies, and toys of families' deceased children in hopes of luring their spirits back home. After midnight, the living stay up to fill the dead in on all the things they've missed since the last meeting. As the spirits of the adult dead return to the world of the living, candy and toys are replaced with atole (a corn-based beverage) and alcohol, and grave sites are adorned with flowers, lit candles, and incense.

The festival itself is an interesting blend of Catholic and Indigenous traditions. The Spanish conquest in the sixteenth century saw the forceful intro-duction of the Catholic festivals of All Saints' Day and All Souls' Day, which eventually melded with existing rituals of ancestor worship, despite the criminalization of pagan rituals in the mid-1700s.[35] Many of the most enduring symbols of Día de los

Muertos—the incense, the offerings of flowers, and the proliferation of skeletons—hearken back to Mexico's precolonial Mesoamerican past, when the polytheistic civilizations of the Aztecs, Mayas, and Olmecs (among others) worshipped a pantheon full of skeletal death gods. They also passed on their belief that the dead could retain a powerful hold over the living; it was understood that the dead had the means to intercede with the gods on the living's behalf or send down devastating plagues, so it was best to get on their good side. The living did this in much the same way as Mexicans do today: by honoring the dead through festivals and offering up gifts of food and flowers.[36]

In the words of Mexican poet Octavio Paz, where the Westerner shudders at the thought of death, the Mexican "frequents it, mocks it, caresses it, sleeps with it, entertains it; it is one of his favorite playthings and his most enduring love."[37] Today, Mexico's culture is a preeminent example of one that does not shy away from confronting human mortality, engaging with it publicly and turning it into a communal experience.

Death Lives at Home

Mexico isn't the only place that welcomes the dead back into the abodes of the living. Many Asian, African, and Indigenous cultures all over the world still practice what is popularly known as ancestor worship, wherein spirits of the familial dead are invoked and communed with on a regular basis. Oftentimes, the relationship between the living and the dead is reciprocal— the dead are revered as gods and plied with offerings of food and prayer, all the while serving as spiritual guides, heavenly disciplinarians, and bringers of luck and fortune. The altars upon which they are honored frequently serve as loci of memory, spaces that allow for devotees to come to terms with their place in the world by engaging with their lineage.

Mexico

Central to the Mexican Day of the Dead is the erection of an ofrenda, or "offering"; set up by family members of the deceased, it serves as a place for collective grief, celebration, and remembrance. Many altars have three tiers that represent heaven, earth, and the underworld, though more elaborate ones can boast as many as seven tiers.

Almost every object that adorns the altar, from the perfumed smoke of copal incense to the vibrant (and pungent) marigolds, serves to lure the dead back home. Water is left to purify the dead and quench their thirst. It is, as many Latin American rituals are, an exercise in syncretism: Pre-Hispanic customs are carried out under the watchful eye of the Virgin Mary and her crucified son. Food is plentiful—a tradition that comes from the Indigenous belief that spirits of the dead grow hungry on their long journeys back to the mortal plane.[38]

1. Decorated tablecloth or serape (draped over the table)

2. Religious icons on the uppermost level

3. Photos of the dead

4. Candles

5. Chalice containing copal incense

6. A cup or bowl of water

7. Cempasúchils, or Mexican marigolds— the so-called flor de muerto (flower of the dead)

8. Sweets, fruits, loaves of bread known as pan de muerto, and the deceased's favorite foods

9. Sugar skulls, papel picado (decorative paper crafts), and calacas (skeletal figurines)

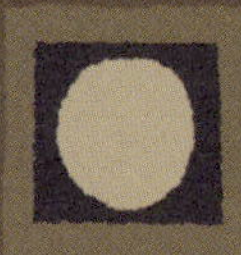

芳　流　德
祖德綿長百世昌
神恩普遍三多佶

China

For many Chinese people, the dead aren't just visiting spirits invoked on special holidays. Spirits are housed year-round in altars that vary in style, ranging from traditional altar tables and cabinets to ones that look like miniature houses. There, they're revered alongside a god or deity of the family's choosing, one that is usually picked on the merit of their divine strengths—Guan Yin for a long and peaceful life, for example, or Guan Gong for his strength and courage. Much care is taken regarding the altar's placement, and it is considered both auspicious and respectful to rest it against a solid wall in a well-lit room. In accordance with the rules of feng shui, an altar should never face a staircase, a bedroom or bathroom door, or a long hallway, lest you disrupt the flow of energy throughout the house.[39]

Many keep altars in the home out of concern for the dead's spiritual welfare, as well as out of a sense of familial duty.[40] In a culture so dominated by Confucian ideals, it may be said that these ritual rites are a natural extension of the hierarchical, reverential treatment of elders that already permeates Chinese society.

1. Statues of deities or gods (placed in the center of the altar or on the topmost tier; lesser gods are placed on either side)

2. Incense holder containing sandalwood incense sticks

3. Lotus lamps or electric candle lamps

4. Flowers (white chrysanthemums are always a good choice)

5. Didactic phrases meant to convey values and virtues such as filial piety.

6. Spirit tablet(s) inscribed with the name(s) of the deceased

7. Fresh fruits like apples, oranges, and pineapples—always offered in odd numbers and arranged in a pyramidal structure

Benin

Familial altars were commonplace inside the homes of people across all social strata in the West African Kingdom of Benin (circa 900–1897 CE), but the most impressive were the ones kept by the obas, or kings. Royal altars were primarily kept to ensure dynastic continuity, and it was considered the responsibility of a newly installed oba to build and dedicate one to his father and predecessor, or to his mother if she had obtained the rank of queen mother.

Some objects, like the bells and rattle staffs used to awaken the ancestral dead to prayers offered on their behalf, were common on all ancestral altars kept by the Edo people of Benin. Others, like the intricately carved ivory tusks showing scenes of transformation, war, or ritual,[41] or the life-size brass heads depicting past kings, were specific to royal altars. On account of its resistance to corrosion, brass was an important symbol of kingship, and its production was so strictly controlled that anyone found casting brass without royal approval risked execution.[42] It was believed that the spirits of the dead provided protection to both the king and the state, and the royal altar was regularly activated with offerings of food or blood.

Though the kingdom collapsed in 1897 after its brutal annexation by the British, many of these rituals continue to be practiced today in the modern city of Benin in Nigeria.[43]

1. Carved elephant tusks

2. Rattle staffs[44]

3. Brass bells

4. Cast copper alloy heads representing an oba[45]

5. Bronze figurines

Korea

In Korea, home altars are periodically set up to conduct highly elaborate ceremonies such as jesa (which is typically only performed at night, on death anniversaries) and charye (which is performed in the day) on happier occasions like Lunar New Year and Chuseok—a festival of thanksgiving where families gather to thank their ancestors for a good harvest. Charye is traditionally performed for the last four generations of one's family and often requires the preparation of anywhere from twenty to thirty dishes that are arranged and served in a manner that is often incredibly specific, though the kinds of dishes presented can differ depending on the region (you'll find more seafood in coastal cities like Busan, for instance).[46] Incense is lit to mark the start (and end) of the ceremony, upon which alcohol is offered to the ancestors of those gathered by holding a cup above the incense and swirling it thrice clockwise. Following the presentation of alcohol, family members bow twice—an action reserved solely for the dead (as opposed to bowing once, which is for the living). The dishes are "served" to the dead in a ritual ceremony, after which the food is eaten and enjoyed by those who have gathered.

The charye ritual is currently facing a moment of reckoning: The meal often takes days to prepare, a burden that is, traditionally, shouldered entirely by the women of the family. Some view these formalities as being oppressively rigid, and many have instead opted for smaller commemorative gatherings with family—some in rebellion against outmoded gender expectations, and others simply out of convenience.[47]

1. A screen or shinwi (memorial tablet)

2. First row: rice, tteokguk (rice cake soup, served on Lunar New Year and replaced with songpyeon—another type of rice cake—during Chuseok), and utensils

3. Second row, from left to right: guksu (noodles), yukjeon (meat pancakes), yukjeok (grilled beef), sojeok (pan-fried skewers), eojeok (fish that, if served whole, is traditionally arranged so its face looks east and its tail west), and eojeon (fish pancakes)

4. Third row: meat, beef, and fish soup

5. Fourth row: po (jerky), namul (seasoned vegetables), nabak kimchi, ganjang (soy sauce), and sikhye (a sweet rice punch)

6. Fifth row: fruits and desserts such as dates, chestnuts, Korean pears, persimmons, apples, and desserts such as hangwa, traditionally arranged in this order

7. Incense with incense burner

Dead Ringer

In the West, the idea of speaking with the dead usually brings to mind images of Ouija boards, bloodied women in mirrors, ghost hunters, and other things often dismissed as party games or pseudoscience. But such was the basis on which Spiritualism, an American movement centered around communicating with the dead, was founded. Popularized in the wake of the Civil War by the Fox sisters (Maggie, Kate, and Leah) from Hydesville, New York, Spiritualism works at the intersection of science, mysticism, and religion—a formula that proved to be such a hit with the general public that it eventually spread to Britain, where it quickly established itself in the mainstream in the second half of the nineteenth century.

The Fox sisters were mediums—from the Latin *medius*, meaning "middle"—who served as intermediaries between the living and the dead. They traveled extensively, holding séances and interpreting ghostly messages using what they called a "spiritual telegraph," which entailed the interpretation of knocks supposedly made by phantoms who had been called upon to appear. Ghosts made their presence known in different ways: Some levitated furniture, possessed mediums who had entered trancelike states, or, most famously, caused Spiritualists to expel a substance known as ectoplasm. Taken from the Greek words *ektos* and *plasma* (as in "outside formed"), ectoplasm was a white fluid that emanated from the medium's body (most often through their mouths), and it would then come to life and take shape before its audience.[48] At the height of Spiritualism's popularity in the nineteenth century, thousands flocked into dark rooms to participate in séances, for which they sat gathered with their hands touching. Some sessions took place in cabinets where the medium was obscured from the sitter, ostensibly to prove that they could engender all manner of phenomena without any outside help.

Regardless, skeptics continued to discount the movement, claiming it to be an industry populated with hucksters and con artists who were all too willing to scam the grieving public out of their hard-earned dollars. Vocal critics included the famed illusionist and escape artist Harry Houdini, who ferociously and publicly exposed fraudulent mediums he saw to be transgressing on the ethics and artistry of his craft. In the last months of his life, he appeared before Congress to testify in support of criminalizing commercial fortune-telling, as well as "any person pretending to . . . unite the separated."[49]

Houdini's suspicions were not unfounded; after she was offered a bribe in 1888, Maggie Fox confessed that she and her sisters had faked the knocks heard in their séances by cracking the joints of their toes. Ectoplasm, Spiritualism's iconic symbol, looked a lot like cheesecloth in the light.

The bad press generated by frequent exposés eventually led to the decline of Spiritualism in the early 1900s. But it wasn't all bad. The movement granted the mediums, who were very often female, an unprecedented amount of financial freedom and independence that had thus far been closed off to them.[50] For those who participated, the rituals gave them something immediate and tangible toward which they could direct their grief, promising closure for both the living and the dead. In any case, the idea of our souls living on after death, guiding the people we love and leave behind, is simply too enticing to ever be banished completely from the collective imagination.[51] The presence of someone like a medium—that is, a person who practices spiritual invocation (inviting a spirit to possess someone) and evocation (getting a spirit to appear in a specific location)—is also common throughout various animistic and Indigenous cultures. The Sámi peoples of northern Europe asked shamans

Curious Coffins and Riveting Rituals

known as noaidis to intercede with spirits in order to ensure favorable hunts and good health, while in Nepal, jhākris brandish drums called dhyāngros to invoke ancestral ghosts. In Korea, mudangs (possessed shamans) and seseummu (shamans who inherit their gifts) answer their spiritual calling by undergoing a ritual initiation known as "spirit sickness," where they are called in to intercede in all manner of spiritual problems, from exorcisms to fortune-telling.[52]

Though Spiritualism never regained its initial popularity, séances are still conducted by Spiritualists today. There is a reason why Spiritualism attracted such a large following in the first place: Despite its colorful history of scams and scandals, the catharsis it provided was often very real. In the words of noted Spiritualist Sir Arthur Conan Doyle (who himself had many public clashes with his friend Houdini): "The final argument for the truth of our new revelation is that it is the most natural, reasonable, and comforting interpretation of the facts of human life and destiny which has ever been put forward. It is huge, sweeping, all-explaining, reaching out to all our difficulties, and giving adequate answers."[53] In other words, if it brought you comfort, well, maybe it was true enough.

Famous Phantoms

Ghosts, as we have conceived of them in our folklore and urban legends, are often spirits with unfinished business that keeps them tethered to this world. At once a reminder of our mortality and a promise that death is not the end, ghosts and spirits, both benign and malicious, appear across many different cultural narrative traditions. From the disembodied spirits of murdered women, hell-bent on exacting their revenge upon the living, to the mischievous child ghosts that play tricks on the living until they are baptized or buried, many archetypal ghosts serve to uphold moralizing ideals for the living in their depiction of human (and especially female) suffering.[54]

The Wild Hunt

Popular in the folklore of northern Europe, this horde of spectral hunters or warriors on horseback is usually engaged in a chase and led by some historical figure or another.

The Pontianak

Also known as the Kuntilanak across parts of Southeast Asia, she is believed to be the ghost of a woman who died in childbirth and seeks to do harm to men, pregnant women, and young children. She is often accompanied by the scent of frangipani flowers or the sound of an infant crying. During the day, she is said to sleep in banana trees.

Dybbuk

A malicious possessive ghost from Jewish folklore that attaches itself to a host—usually someone who has fallen ill—until it is exorcised. Belief in dybbuks was particularly widespread in the seventeenth century among German and Polish Jews.

Curious Coffins and Riveting Rituals

Mylings

Also known as utburds (from a Norse word meaning "that which is taken outside"), these were believed to be the ghosts of children left unburied or unbaptized. According to Norwegian folklore, they are prone to assaulting lone wanderers by jumping onto their backs and demanding they be carried to a graveyard to be buried in consecrated ground.

La Llorona

Her name means "the weeping woman," and this vengeful ghost from Mexican folklore haunts areas in and around bodies of water, mourning the children she drowned in a jealous rage upon discovering her husband's adultery.

Funayūrei

Groups of these figures from Japanese mythology, believed to be the ghosts of people who drowned at sea, are said to appear to sailors and fishermen on foggy or stormy days in hopes of drowning them too.

Dust to Dust

A common fear shared by people all over (and indeed the driving force behind most of our beliefs and rituals around death) is the prospect of meaning so little to others that we will be abandoned and forgotten after we die. We are social creatures, so it's probably unsurprising that many can conceive of no greater misfortune than being completely disconnected from one's own community. Many of our rituals of remembrance sate our desire for community and continuance. After all, to be forgotten is to become nothing, and to be no one—the loneliest kind of death there is.

This, of course, begs the question: Who remembers the indigent dead? The unhoused and destitute, who often die cut off from any kind of support structure, lie unclaimed in the morgues before they are at last disposed of in anonymous burials. Traditionally, the state foots the bill for the funerals and burial rites of those with no traceable family, or with families too poor to afford death services. In England, these funerals are sometimes referred to as pauper's funerals, which came into being in the nineteenth century to address the growing needs of workers living in abject poverty. Most of them are no-frills services, conducted without ceremony.[55] Just as the well-appointed funerals of the rich and influential signified their place in the upper crust of society, the ignoble funerals of the poor signaled the opposite—what historian Thomas W. Laqueur refers to as "their absolute exclusion from the social body."[56]

Traditionally, the indigent dead were buried in potter's fields, so called after the biblical account of priests using the money Judas received for his betrayal of Jesus to purchase a clay-rich field in which to bury the unknown dead. However, in recent years, cremations have mostly upended the practice. This is the fate that awaits thousands of the United States' unhoused dead, whose ashes are sometimes kept on shelves for years, waiting to be claimed. Most never are. Los Angeles counts in its annual census upward of about seventy-five thousand unhoused people, a number that has only continued to rise in recent years.[57] There are more unhoused people—and more unhoused dead—in this one city than in Chicago, San Francisco, and New York combined.[58] Most die in complete anonymity, but commemorative events like Homeless Persons' Memorial Day, held on December 21 (the day of the winter solstice and the longest night of the year), are growing in popularity. Events often include the holding of candlelight vigils, moments of silence, and the reading of names—all of them carried out, quite fittingly, in the bitter cold.[59]

During the Hungry Ghost Festival (page 133), street altars are frequently dedicated to the anonymous dead, due to the Taoist belief that the hungry, malevolent ghosts born of the neglect or desertion of one's elders must be appeased, lest misfortune, illness, or even death befall anyone caught in their path.[60] In Japan, Buddhist monks sometimes honor the nameless dead, lighting incense and praying for the souls of everyone who has died on a particular day. They remember the dead, even if no one else does.[61]

The practical need to get rid of dead bodies as cost-efficiently as possible often runs in parallel with the communal obligation to provide everyone, regardless of social status and wealth, some dignity in death. In laying the unclaimed bodies of the destitute dead to rest in a manner that affords them some basic decency and respect, commemorative rituals also call to our attention all the ways in which the system fails its most vulnerable citizens while they live and breathe.

Funerary Monuments

Enduring Eternity

In most cases, the people history remembers are those at the very top of the food chain. Say you've led a storied life: You've conquered civilizations, come to exert massive amounts of influence over the hearts and minds of your people, and have amassed a near-unlimited supply of cold, hard cash. You've become a real *somebody*—somebody worth remembering even centuries after you've shuffled off this mortal coil. Humanity, as previously discussed, has a long and varied history of performing rituals of remembrance, but what is equally true is that we are fickle, forgetful creatures, inconveniently prone to dying off ourselves. Even embalming bodies does not preserve them forever; it merely delays the unstoppable process of decay. If you *really* want to be remembered, you leave behind something that lasts.

The death of a person can completely alter the social landscape of a community, so it seems only natural that its physical one should change as well. The compulsion to leave a lasting and tangible mark in the world of the living is yet another cross-cultural occurrence. It is also one we share with our ancient ancestors; prehistoric monuments such as tumuli (which are essentially mounds of

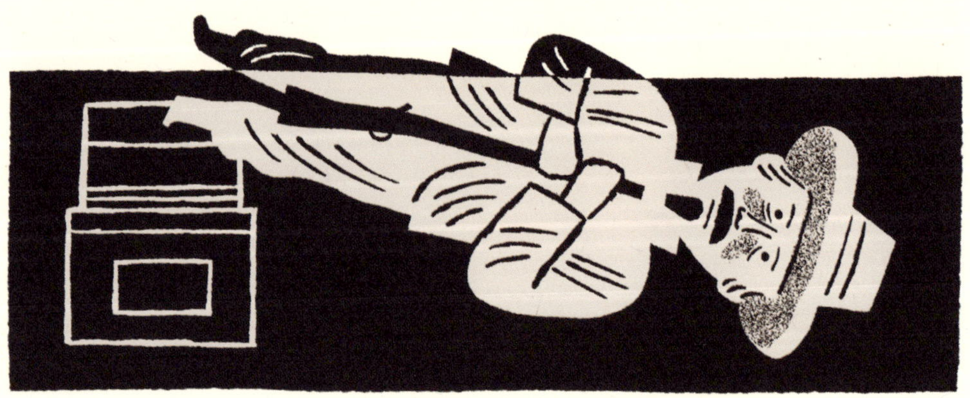

earth and stone), dolmens (which are tablelike monuments), and other megaliths have been found throughout Europe and Asia, with some dating back to around 4500 BCE.[62] These days, makeshift public memorials still frequently spring up at sites of tragedy, and many graves across cultures are capped with headstones, crosses, and other burial markers intended to signify to those who stumble across them that, yes, you existed, and you had a name.

But while many funerary monuments are put up with the intention of having them endure for eternity, the ones that tend to stick around are usually those built to commemorate the wealthy, powerful, and publicly revered, although they can differ greatly in terms of scale and function. While simple tombs and gravestones can serve as sites for both private and public rituals of remembrance, public monuments almost always deal in the latter. They are usually constructed out of stone, metal,

or another such material prized for its durability, and they are often incredibly ornate, or so large as to be nearly indestructible. Many of them require so much time and money to build that construction starts before the demise of the people they are meant to commemorate. The Pyramids of Giza, for instance, were commissioned by the very people they were built to entomb, thereby allowing the pharaohs to actively shape how they would be remembered. Some of today's tallest and most iconic structures are monuments dedicated to the dead, including colossal mortuary complexes such as the Taj Mahal. In addition to their sheer size, funerary monuments tend to occupy prominent places in our cities, towns, and parks. Many are erected in places that already hold some significance to the surrounding population, or in spaces specifically designed to accommodate them. In short, these things are pretty hard to miss. And therein lies the point—public monuments to the dead do not rely on personal grief or incidental reverie to evoke memories of the people they commemorate. Monuments, many of them so enduring and recognizable that they can sometimes come to represent entire civilizations, serve first and foremost as sites of collective memory, where figures of importance are used to educate a community about its shared history, legitimize the powers that be, and uphold the allegorical ideals of the state or society.

When the light hits just right in Giza, Egypt, the city literally lives in the shadow of death. In places like this, the historical dead aren't relegated to the fringes of social life—they're embedded right in the physical and spiritual fabric of daily life.

Set in Stone

In the good ol' days, before print, photography, and the internet forever changed the way we share and consume visual information, the preferred method of image production and dissemination for the ruling class was the production of statues—sculptural representations of one's likeness, wrought in stone or bronze and, by virtue of size or placement, designed for maximum visibility. From the life-size statues of artists, writers, and scientists that pepper our public spaces to the colossal statues of politicians and kings that loom (or loomed) over town squares, statues have long served as objects of worship, tools of mass propaganda, and markers of prestige and recognition.

Most striking are the colossal statues of statesmen erected in various parts of the world, such as those found in countries once part of the now-defunct Soviet Union. Excessive as they may seem today, colossal statues—from the Greek *kolossoi*, first used by Herodotus to describe the hulking stone visages of Egyptian pharaohs[63]—have a clear historical precedent. As mentioned, pharaonic Egypt was filled to the brim with colossal funerary statues, such as the pair of colossi depicting the pharaoh Amenhotep III, which stand (well, sit) guard in front of the ruins of his mortuary temple. The Greeks were no strangers to colossal statues either, though most of theirs were of gods such as Zeus and Athena. Although most colossal statues have historically been depictions of religious figures, the tallest statue standing today is the 597-foot-tall Statue of Unity commemorating Vallabhbhai Patel, one of the key architects of modern India.

In other cases, the dead make themselves known not by sheer scale but by simply being everywhere at once. In the early days of imperial Rome, it was virtually impossible for the average Roman citizen to go about their daily life without encountering imperial portraits of the empire's founder, Gaius Octavius Thurinus, better known to history as Augustus. Aside from handling coins that bore his portrait, laypeople would've been exposed to statues bearing his likeness in town squares, temples, basilicas, and theaters.[64] Through the careful management of his sculpted image, Augustus died a deified god-king, effectively codifying in the West a method for legitimizing one's rule by literally setting one's visage in stone. Statues from antiquity informed many of the public works that were erected throughout the 1800s and now make up a bulk of the extant monuments in our plazas, near our important buildings, and in our city parks.

Today, the commemoration of anyone, living or dead, through the medium of statuary is nowhere near as common an impulse as it was one to two hundred years ago. The statues that are put up these days tend to be of figures from popular culture (think athletes, pop stars, and entertainers) or of figures from historically marginalized communities in an effort to level the majority-white-and-male playing field.[65] Statues, in their consistent and prolonged association with the ruling class, are inherently political. When a person is honored with one, it is always a public statement; it doesn't really matter whether or not you know anything about their lives, so long as you know that they are important.

Monumental Change

But how do we decide who deserves to be commemorated? Who gets to choose?

In the wake of the civil unrest following the 2020 murder of George Floyd, hundreds of statues linked to racial injustice and violence were taken down all over the world—often forcibly, and occasionally against state law. One by one, statues of slave owners, Confederate generals, and brutal colonizer-kings were defaced, toppled, and dumped in various bodies of water. In Belgium, a bust of King Leopold II was removed from a park for his role in the atrocities committed in the Congo. A bronze statue of transatlantic slave trader Edward Colston was torn down by protesters in Bristol, England. And all throughout the United States, memorials associated with white supremacy, racism, and slavery were brought low, including those of Confederate general Robert E. Lee and US presidents George Washington and Thomas Jefferson, who each owned hundreds of slaves.

One critic decried their removal as being tantamount to "whitewashing our history, turning our heads away from the inconvenient truths of our past,"[66] and opponents of the movement argued that such statues should be left alone to serve as reminders of the nation's heritage, no matter how complicated. It was a reckoning unlike any other seen in recent history, but just as how putting up statues is a time-honored tradition, so is tearing them down.

The story of iconoclasm—originally referring to the destruction of religious icons throughout the Byzantine Empire but since expanded to include all forms of art and cultural artifacts—is one heard and told across the world.[67] There seems to be a recurring compulsion to destroy images in moments of cultural and political change whenever commemorative techniques become outmoded or the legacies of their subjects are called into scrutiny. Statues of Communist Party leaders were taken down after the collapse of the Soviet Union, and the visages of pharaohs were defaced by invaders and successors alike; commemorative statues of the dead are erected with eternity in mind, but they can often become the political battlegrounds on which culture wars are waged.

Gary Younge put it best: "This statue obsession mistakes adulation for history, history for heritage and heritage for memory. It attempts to detach the past from the present, the present from morality, and morality from responsibility."[68] History, unlike these unchanging symbols of reverence, is not set in stone. As a society reevaluates who is worthy of commemoration, perhaps the radical act of removing statues is precisely the push we need to confront the ghosts of our past.

What's in a Name?

Few things are as closely tied to our identities as our names. The urge to christen the places and geographical features we live in and around is hardwired into our DNA: Since time immemorial, we've been naming the rivers, mountains, and valleys on which we depend for survival. We do this partly out of a need for stable points of reference, but also because names are instrumental in creating a sense of belonging.[69] Like public monuments, commemorative place-names bring the figures of the past back into the very fabric of daily life, imbuing each space with memory and meaning.

But like all other modes of public commemoration, the art of naming can be charged with social and political tension. Place-names have long been used to legitimize and propagate ideas of political and dynastic authority. Countless town squares and streets bear the names of kings and military leaders, as well as of political ideals like "revolution" and "liberty"—all of which serve to commemorate people, events, or ideas that are seen as part of what sociologist Barry Schwartz calls "a register of sacred history."[70] As such, it has not been uncommon for place-names to change following moments of political disruption or upheaval. Such was the case for the Reichskanzlerplatz of West Berlin: So named after the Imperial Chancellor of Germany (or Reichskanzler), it was renamed Adolf-Hitler-Platz after the Nazis seized power. It reverted back to its original name after the Nazis fell, then changed yet again to Theodor-Heuss-Platz in honor of the first president of the Federal Republic of Germany.[71]

Place-names can feel almost mundane compared with the flashy theatrics of colossal monuments, and chances are that you don't think twice about the dead guy your street is named after. But therein lies the power—commemorative names aren't there to inspire cultlike fervor or to elicit uncontrollable displays of grief. They are there to declare and affirm an "official" version of history,[72] made inseparable from the daily reality of those still alive to see and speak it.

But what happens when the story behind a name is one of violence and omittance? For many marginalized communities, encountering spaces named after people responsible for the colonization, murder, and brutalization of their forebears can serve as just another reminder of the quiet, everyday complicity of the unquestioning public in upholding an unjust system. But these names can, and have begun to, change. To date, the federal government of the United States has renamed hundreds of mountains, lakes, and other geographical features, doing away with their racist or derogatory names. Change seldom came easily, though; when the US Board on Geographic Names agreed to change the name of South Dakota's Harney Peak (so named for US general William S. Harney, nicknamed Woman Killer by the Lakota Sioux for his particular brand of brutality) to Black Elk Peak after the Lakota spiritual leader following nearly fifty years of campaigning, Governor Dennis Daugaard released a statement rebuking the change. He claimed that the renaming of a landmark as prominent as this one not only sowed confusion but also wasted state funds, adding that he suspected that "very few people know the history of either Harney or Black Elk."[73] But, of course, names have power, and the ability to occupy and lay claim to places deemed familiar and significant is often central to people's stories, lived experiences, and emotional well-being.[74] For communities that have long been sidelined, oppressed, and otherwise erased from the annals of history, the act of commemorative naming can be a powerful measure of vindication and recognition. For Myron Pourier, a direct descendent of Black Elk, the push to rename the peak "was never about the negative" but, rather, rooted in a desire for reconciliation and healing for Indigenous communities.[75]

Commemorative naming isn't just limited to toponymy (the study of place-names); people of stature have been honored in a huge variety of ways, lending their names to everything from schools and stars to scholarships and charitable organizations. On a more personal note, many people are named after grandparents or people who have passed—other loved ones or perhaps even admired historical figures. All of us with surnames are the product of a long conga line of people passing on their names to their children, their children's children, and so on.[76] You are a living, breathing extension of all the lives that have come before you, and part of them lives on in you.

Known unto God

On the flip side, sometimes memorials are put up for victims who are, for one reason or another, unnamed. This is common with monuments dedicated to the countless lost or unidentified victims of war, including the Tomb of the Unknown Soldier.

Tombs dedicated to fallen soldiers were popularized in the wake of World War I, which resulted in military casualties on an unprecedented scale. Many of these tombs bear architectural similarities to the tombs and temples of ancient Egypt and classical antiquity, and symbols of purity and eternal remembrance, such as the eternal flame that hearkens back to the legendary fire that burned in the Temple of Apollo in Delphi, are also frequently employed.[77] Some of these tombs are functioning sites of interment, while others (called cenotaphs) are merely symbolic and thus hold no bodies; the tomb in Arlington, Virginia, comprises four crypts and enshrines three unidentified bodies, from World War I, World War II, and the Korean War. The last crypt is kept empty in remembrance of missing soldiers who served in Vietnam.[78] Whether or not they contain human remains, these monuments often serve as stand-ins for the entire military force and are powerful symbols of the loss, sacrifice, waste, and heroism that characterize armed conflicts. They are often the sites of heavily ritualized military ceremonies, including the elaborate changing of the guard—which, in the United States' capital of Washington, DC, is performed by members of a regiment known as the Old Guard, who have watched over the Tomb of the Unknown Soldier every minute of every day since 1937. The ceremony involves a flurry of symbolic gestures representing the 21-gun salute, the highest symbolic military honor that can be bestowed, and is conducted every hour (or half hour, depending on the month).[79] Tombs frequently host foreign dignitaries and heads of state on holidays like Memorial or Veterans Day as a gesture of respect and goodwill between previously warring nations. That the people commemorated at these monuments are unknown does little to diminish the emotional resonance of the spaces; in fact, it is perhaps their anonymity that precisely exemplifies what makes war such a tragedy.

① Tomb of the Unknown Warrior in London, England

Located in Westminster Abbey, this tomb commemorates an unknown soldier brought in from France to be buried in 1920. The idea for this tomb of the unknown is said to have come from Reverend David Railton, a military chaplain who had been serving on the Western Front when he noticed a backyard grave marked with a rough cross on which someone had penciled "An Unknown British Soldier."[80]

② Tomb of the Unknown Soldier in Paris, France

Located under the Arc de Triomphe, the entombed body was buried contemporaneously with its British counterpart in memory of all the soldiers who have died in the name of France throughout the country's history.[81]

③ Tomb of the Unknown Soldier in Rome, Italy

Entombed is the body of an unknown soldier who served in World War I; he was chosen from eleven bodies by a woman from Trieste, who had herself been chosen to represent all Italian mothers who had lost their sons in war.[82]

④ Monument to the Unknown Soldier in Baghdad, Iraq

Dedicated to the unnamed martyrs of the Iran-Iraq War (1980–1988), the monument depicts a falling dira'a, a traditional shield, slipping from the grasp of a dying Iraqi warrior.[83]

⑤ Tomb of the Unknown Soldier in Athens, Greece

The tomb, guarded by evzones (presidential guards) who change by the hour, is dedicated to the soldiers who died serving in World War II and other recent conflicts. The walls contain a relief sculpture depicting a dying Greek soldier, as well as quotes from Thucydides's *History of the Peloponnesian War*.

The Old Lie

"Dulce et Decorum Est," Wilfred Owen's famous wartime poem describing the horrors of World War I, takes its name from (and systematically dismantles) a line in Horace's *Odes*. In full, the original quote reads: "Dulce et decorum est pro patria mori" (It is sweet and proper to die for one's country). War has always been associated with both heroism and horror, and all architects tasked with building wartime monuments face the same challenge posed to countless historians, writers, documentarians, and journalists before them: How do you truthfully represent war? In contrast with the majestic neoclassical tombs dedicated to fallen patriots, memorials dedicated to the victims of human atrocities can take on a much more unconventional look. It is hard to express the sheer scale and horror of genocide, war, and mass terrorism, so memorials dedicated to their countless victims can look very abstract.

The Memorial to the Murdered Jews of Europe (see following pages) consists of 2,711 concrete slabs of varying heights, which form an abstract, wavelike shape no matter where you stand. The memorial is accompanied by an underground museum containing the biographies and names of some of the victims, along with farewell letters, videos, and photographs. Situated in the middle of Berlin, the site bears witness to the state-sponsored persecution and murder of the roughly six million Jews killed in the Holocaust. Conceived by American architect Peter Eisenman, the Field of Stelae is intentionally ambiguous, and visitors are invited to quietly and respectfully contemplate the tragedy however they wish. Some liken the site to a graveyard full of unmarked graves, others to tombs or coffins. But the point of it all is arguably not what the monument looks like but, rather, how it makes you feel. Eisenman has said that "you cannot represent that

which defies description." The site is a disorientating and claustrophobic maze, which he hoped would serve as a pale proxy for the trauma of being held in a concentration camp.[84]

Another similarly abstract site of remembrance is the Vietnam Veterans Memorial in Washington, DC (see art on facing page), which honors fallen US servicepeople who served and died in the conflict. The structure consists of two large, conjoined granite walls engraved, in chronological order, with the names of more than fifty-eight thousand servicepeople who gave their lives fighting in the Vietnam War.[85] The war has a complicated legacy—the first American war to be widely televised, it was long, bloody, and deeply divisive. In its abstraction, the memorial seemingly neither supports nor opposes the war, focusing instead on its many victims. At the same time, its somber color and frank recitation of the lives stolen thousands of miles away may be taken as a condemnation in and of itself. And, indeed, in contrast with the white marble monuments that fill the rest of the National Mall, the Wall, as it is known, stands out like an open wound, a black gash cut right into the earth.

When both of these memorials were unveiled to the public (the Field of Stelae in 2005 and the Vietnam Veterans Memorial in 1982), their reception was decidedly mixed. Perhaps owing to their unconventional nature, there was a widespread perception that in their abstraction, neither gave the events they were commemorating what was owed. Some found the vagueness of the Holocaust memorial in Berlin—whose Field of Stelae named neither the victims nor their murderers—disturbing.[86] The Wall was criticized by some for lacking a human touch, while others took issue with how it sank into the ground when every other monument rose up into the sky.[87] Proponents of both memorials have exalted their virtues in the face of these critiques. Such so-called anti-monuments often end up being more participatory than prescriptive. When you're engaging with abstraction, meaning is not handed to you—you're actively making it yourself. With the Vietnam Veterans Memorial, viewers, friends, and family members of the deceased are literally reflected in the polished black granite behind the names of the dead; when you engage with this memorial and others like it, you are brought into the past in empathy and solidarity.

In "How to Tell a True War Story," Vietnam War veteran Tim O'Brien writes: "A true war story is never moral. It does not instruct, nor encourage virtue, nor suggest models of proper human behavior, nor restrain men from doing the things men have always done. If a story seems moral, do not believe it. If at the end of a war story you feel uplifted, or if you feel that some small bit of rectitude has been salvaged from the larger waste, then you have been made the victim of a very old and terrible lie." While many anti-memorials dedicated to the victims of anthropogenic disasters may appear morally neutral, it is important to remember that sometimes, the most powerful act of condemnation and resistance is to simply lay bare the truth.

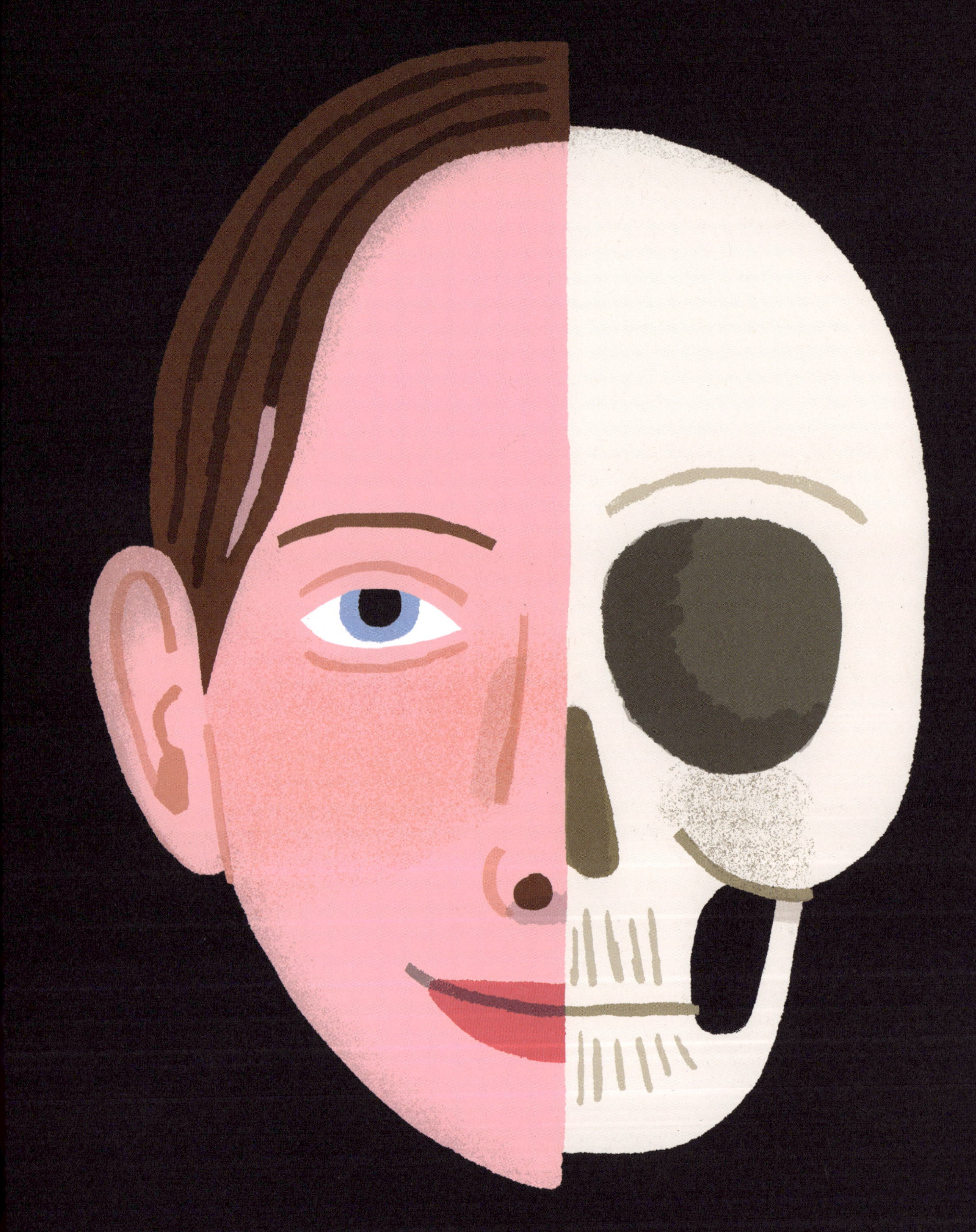

Living

NOTES ON DYING

"In the midst of life, we are in death."
—MEDIA VITA IN MORTE SUMUS, A GREGORIAN CHANT

A Beginner's Guide to Dying

In the words of James Baldwin, life is tragic "simply because the earth turns and the sun inexorably rises and sets, and one day, for each of us, the sun will go down for the last, last time. Perhaps the whole root of our trouble, the human trouble, is that we will sacrifice all the beauty of our lives, will imprison ourselves in totems, taboos, crosses, blood sacrifices, steeples, mosques, races, armies, flags, nations, in order to deny the fact of death, which is the only fact we have."[1]

We start hurtling toward death the moment we're born. Having read this far, you may have been confronted with thoughts about your own demise more than once. Well, join the club. We as a species have been contemplating our mortality since the beginning of time, wrestling with the biggest of questions: How can I die happily, and with dignity? What will happen to me after I draw my last breath? How can I continue to live knowing (or not knowing) what awaits? In many cases, the weight of these questions can lead to a bad case of death anxiety.[2] One of the two most obvious ways this manifests is through avoidance, which itself stems from the belief that death means total annihilation, or perhaps the idea that dying will be a horribly painful experience. Too many hold off on having important conversations about death with their families and friends until it is too late. Some speak of death only euphemistically and spend thousands of dollars on antiaging products, facelifts, and supplements that purport to delay the onset of age. On the flip side, others may be overly cavalier or flippant about death, deflecting their fears with humor or engaging in activities that ostensibly confront or defy death.[3]

For the uninitiated, thinking about death before you're in your death throes may seem morbid or even obsessive. In parts of the world,[4] there is a fear that accepting death, thinking about it, or talking about it invites further misfortune or, at the very least, prevents us from enjoying life's pleasures. But the opposite is true. Denying death doesn't make it go away. If anything, it makes us even more stressed. Throughout history, the creation of memento mori—the reminders of death presented in crypts, paintings of wilting flowers and fruit, and festivals featuring skulls both real and illustrated—were intended not to elicit a traumatic reaction but, rather, to serve the greater goal of memento vitae (reminders of life). In a collection of essays, the fourteenth-century Japanese monk Yoshida Kenkō made the following reference to the cremation grounds of Toribeyama, near Kyoto: "Were we to live on forever—were the dews of Adashino never to vanish, the smoke on Toribeyama never to fade away—then indeed would men not feel the pity of things. . . . Truly the beauty of life is its uncertainty."[5] Death does not have to take away from life. In fact, oftentimes it is the acceptance of our own mortality that enables us to live more fully.

Many are already working toward accepting the inevitable and are helping others do the same. To date, thousands of Death Cafes have sprung up across more than ninety countries, wherein people—often strangers—gather to talk about death over food and drink.[6] A funeral company in Seoul organizes funerals for the living, where students and retirees alike are invited to craft their last wills and testaments, get their funeral portraits taken, and contemplate death in closed coffins.[7] In the United States, organizations like the Order of the Good Death work to foster a death-positive culture via their vast library of resources as well as legislative advocacy.[8]

So if this is advice you need to hear, I'm happy to give it: It is time to learn how to die. As mortician Caitlin Doughty has repeatedly advised, talk to the people you love about death—theirs, and your own. As much as you can and if you are welcome, show up to rituals conducted for the dead in your community. Do your research on what can or should happen after you die. Spend time with the bodies of your loved ones before they are taken away. Live conscientiously; the Swedish have a custom called döstädning, or "death cleaning," where those close to death prepare their homes by getting rid of all unnecessary objects so as not to burden their loved ones after they die. However, designer and writer Margareta Magnusson stresses that anyone at any age can engage in the practice in order to live more intentionally with the objects they keep close by.[9] We are, after all, only here for a short time.

And you already know how this ends.

The Good Death

While many of us would probably prefer to die in the comfort of our own homes surrounded by the people we love, the simple reality of modern life is that many of us will likely meet our ends in the palliative ward of a hospital or hospice, cared for by strangers.

Much has changed over a few short centuries—throughout much of human history, death happened at home, and as recently as the late 1800s, dying in a hospital was considered the last resort for the poor and downtrodden, who died alone, with no one to help or mourn them.[10] By the early 1900s, we had begun the clear shift toward medicalized death as we know it today, where death has become the purview of health-care institutions and long-term care facilities. In *The Hour of Our Death*, death historian Philippe Ariès describes the last wishes of a dying French peasant in the nineteenth century: After a debilitating bout of cholera lasting four days, she requested that the village priest bring her extreme unction, the Catholic sacrament of anointing the sick with oil and prayer in order to give them comfort and courage. What used to be a familial and spiritual event with occasional medical support has, for many, become a medical event with limited familial or spiritual support. What Ariès refers to as the "nauseating spectacle" of dying—the soiled sheets, incontinence, sweat, and discolored skin—was deemed unfit to exist in civilized society, and death was thus relegated to hospitals, where it would not offend the senses of the living.[11]

Of course, this isn't to wax poetic about the good ol' days of the bubonic plague or the frequently preventable and dismal ways people died before the advent of modern medicine. Human beings are living longer than ever before, and access to lifesaving and pain-reducing care has increased across the board. Hospices, named from the Latin *hospitum*, began as places of rest and refuge for the ill and destitute in fourth-century Europe. When the Crusades rolled around, Christian orders set up hospices along the road to care for injured pilgrims, knights, and soldiers. The first modern hospice, which opened in London in 1967, was founded by British nurse and physician Dame Cicely Saunders on the belief that all people should be granted the care they need to die with love and dignity.[12] This, along with palliative care—the total care of terminal or incurably ill patients—forms the basis of what constitutes end-of-life care today.[13] But there has been a widespread call for change within the medical community: Medical science has advanced at such a rapid pace over the last fifty years that, too often, futile or inappropriate medical treatment is administered near death to ensure health and survival.[14] Some professionals, like surgeon and writer Atul Gawande, are pushing for change. To him, death is not the enemy and should not be resisted, postponed, or avoided at the cost of prolonging the suffering of the patient or their family. In his words, the ultimate goal for any medical professional, and indeed for us all, "is not a good death but a good life to the very end."[15]

Death Becomes Her

Then there is the other aspect of dying that doctors and physicians are often ill-equipped to deal with: caring for the mind and spirit. Death has become increasingly high-tech, and technological advancements have come with a depersonalization that many find disturbing. There will always be a need for a human touch at the end of life; many turn to therapists, patient support groups, or people—often women—known as death doulas. The word *doula* comes from a Greek word meaning "a woman who serves," and it is usually used in reference to women who aid in the process of childbirth. But doulas are also trained to assist those at the end, rather than the start, of life. They are called in to offer their patients company over meals, to listen and commiserate with them, to help them plan their funerals, and to hold vigil as they slip from this world into the next. Francesca Lynn Arnoldy, the original developer of the University of Vermont's end-of-life doula training programs, finds that death and life are similar. "The intensity of it, the mystery, all of the unknowns. You have to relinquish your sense of control and agenda and ride it out."[16]

Counting Down

The circumstances in which one is forced to confront their mortality aren't always ideal. Prisoners on death row face an end unlike anything most of us will ever experience: After a period of incarceration, they must contend with the knowledge that in several weeks (or even several hours),[17] they will be executed. Once widespread, the death penalty is legal in just over fifty countries, though only about eleven have consistently executed people in the last five years—the United States being one of them.[18] As of July 1, 2024, there were 2,216 prisoners facing execution across twenty-eight states; most would be executed via lethal injection.[19]

While the last few months after someone receives their final sentence are perhaps the most harrowing, prisoners can spend anywhere from a few weeks to several decades behind bars awaiting either their execution or the conclusion of lengthy court proceedings. As of July 2024, more than half of American prisoners currently on death row had been counting down for more than eighteen years, many of which they likely spent isolated from other prisoners, granted a fraction of the visitation hours allocated to convicts with lesser sentences, and kept out of prison education and employment programs.[20] During this time, prisoners are suspended in a kind of limbo—alive but otherwise cut off from the normalcy of daily life and denied any kind of direction, agency, or certainty. In many ways, their final days and hours are structured like a kind of ceremony—albeit one shaped by bureaucracy, where input from the prisoners is extremely limited. And it is in this context that many of them must face their mortality, often with only a sliver of the support they would've gotten outside the prison system.

The Final Hours

1. Around three days before the execution date, the prisoner is transferred to a secondary building known as the death house, where they are placed under strict surveillance. Their final days are spent in visitations with attorneys and family members, sometimes behind glass, sometimes not.

2. The prison guards and the execution team start to prepare, and decisions regarding which journalists will be in attendance during the execution are made.

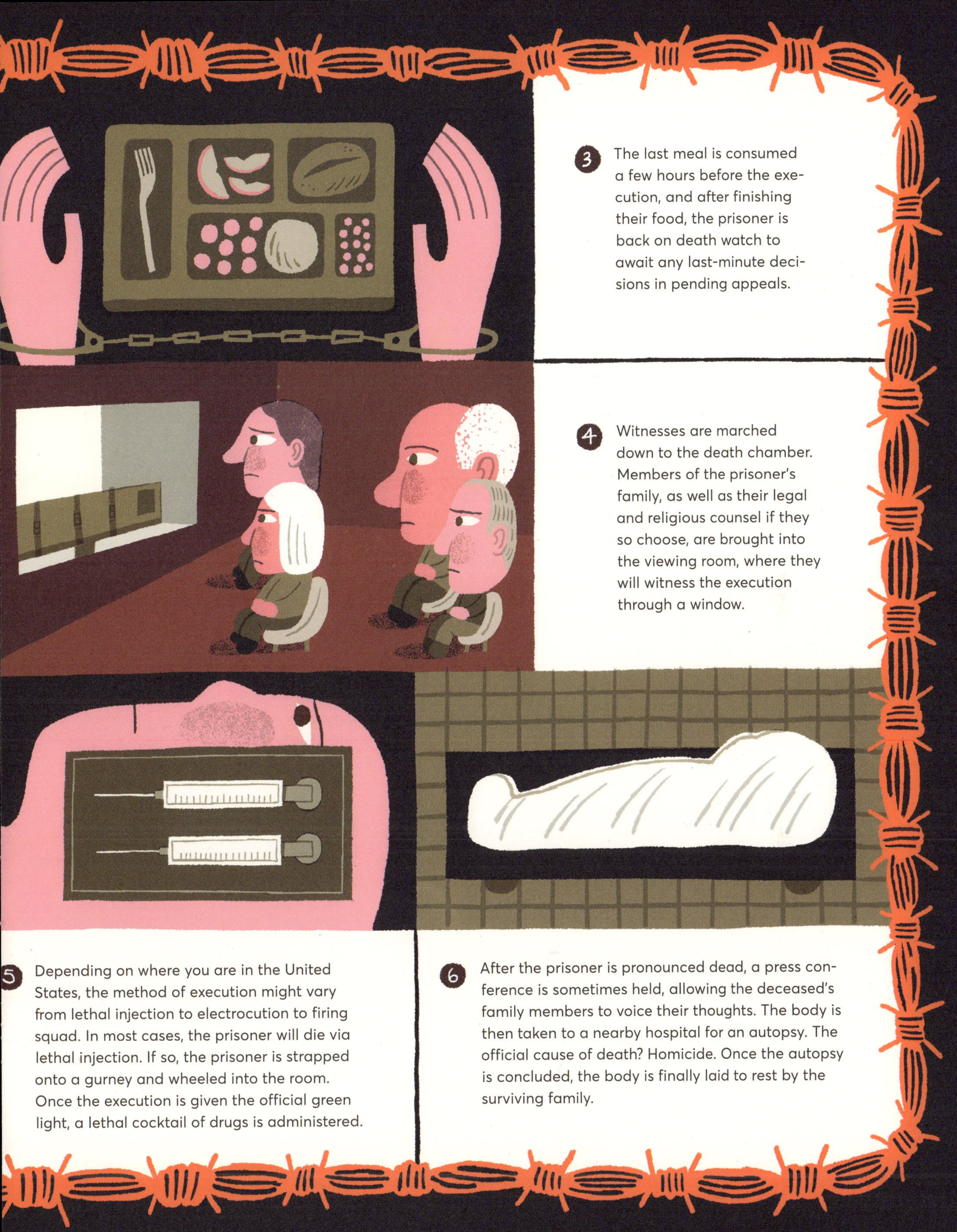

3 The last meal is consumed a few hours before the execution, and after finishing their food, the prisoner is back on death watch to await any last-minute decisions in pending appeals.

4 Witnesses are marched down to the death chamber. Members of the prisoner's family, as well as their legal and religious counsel if they so choose, are brought into the viewing room, where they will witness the execution through a window.

5 Depending on where you are in the United States, the method of execution might vary from lethal injection to electrocution to firing squad. In most cases, the prisoner will die via lethal injection. If so, the prisoner is strapped onto a gurney and wheeled into the room. Once the execution is given the official green light, a lethal cocktail of drugs is administered.

6 After the prisoner is pronounced dead, a press conference is sometimes held, allowing the deceased's family members to voice their thoughts. The body is then taken to a nearby hospital for an autopsy. The official cause of death? Homicide. Once the autopsy is concluded, the body is finally laid to rest by the surviving family.

In a system already considered by many to be oppressively dehumanizing, the final rites granted (or denied) to those awaiting execution can sometimes become heated points of contention, which is exactly what happened in the lead-up to John Henry Ramirez's execution. The then thirty-seven-year-old former marine was scheduled to be executed in 2021 for the robbing and murder of convenience store employee Pablo Castro, and he had asked for his pastor to lay his hands on him as he died—an act meant to provide both comfort and guidance into the afterlife. For Ramirez, who was Baptist, it represented one final opportunity to engage with his faith in the moment when it was most needed.[21] The state denied his request on the grounds of it being a security risk, and he sued them for infringing on his right to religious freedom. What ensued was a wider conversation about prison reform, the ethicality of the death penalty, and prisoner rights at the moment of death. In the end, the court ruled in his favor, holding that states are required to accommodate requests from death row inmates who wish to have their religious counsels pray and touch them during the execution.[22] Though Ramirez was eventually executed in 2022, he died—as much as the system allowed—his way.

The Last Supper

Humans are fascinated by the idea of a last meal. Perhaps it's the discord between the consumption of food—a communal, life-giving activity—and the concept of state-sanctioned death that draws us in. Maybe it's the fact that it's one of the last times a prisoner is acknowledged as an autonomous individual. Or maybe we pay attention because we think the menu reveals something about the psyche of the condemned.[23]

The tradition of the last meal dates back to at least ancient Greece, when people facing execution were fed to prevent their return as hungry ghosts. In eighteenth-century Germany, the Hangman's Meal for the condemned was a large ritualistic dinner party attended by local dignitaries, members of the clergy, and sometimes even the executioner himself. During the dinner, the person who had been sentenced to death was put through a series of scripted exchanges in which they were urged to repent. The meal itself was typically a grand smorgasbord of expensive meats and wine, though there were no guarantees that the condemned would have the appetite to eat any of it.[24] In any

case, the meal was more of a symbolic gesture than anything else, one that united the condemner and the condemned in a ritual of acceptance and forgiveness. Later, the Puritans of Massachusetts held something similar in emulation of the Last Supper of Christ, providing the prisoner and the community with a kind of communal atonement.[25]

But this enigmatic final rite is not a privilege always afforded. When convicted murderer and white supremacist Lawrence Brewer was sentenced to die in the '90s, he ordered a lavish meal of "two chicken-fried steaks, a triple meat bacon cheese-burger, a cheese omelet, fried okra, fajitas, a pint of ice cream, a pound of barbecue with white bread, a pizza, and three root beers." He proceeded to eat none of it. One letter from Senator John Whitmire later, the tradition of requesting a last meal in Texas was abolished.[26] Also, far from the idealized notion that prisoners can order whatever they want, many states have strict budgetary limits, and certain food items, such as alcohol, are rarely permitted.

Pay It Forward

For all this talk about rituals, ghosts, and the afterlife, there are also those who don't much care about what happens after. In fact, as some countries grow increasingly secular, there are many who believe that what awaits us after death . . . is nothing at all. But regardless of our beliefs, this much is true: For the bodies we leave behind, death is only the beginning.

The living will always need dead bodies—whether those bodies are used to further scientific and medical study or to supply organs for transplant, they can positively impact the living in innumerable ways. The history of scientific enlightenment and anatomical study is built on a mountain of corpses, a vast majority of them anonymous and acquired without consent. In sixteenth-century Britain and up until the passing of the Anatomy Act some three hundred years later, the only corpses that schools and anatomists legally had access to were those of executed criminals.[27] In an era so dominated by Christianity, where the spiritual need for full-bodied burials reigned supreme, having one's body carved up by scientists was considered a fate worse than death. Nonetheless, some prisoners not up for dissection would barter with anatomists, trading their postmortem bodies for money in order to afford better clothing to die in.[28] Eventually, the academic demand for bodies began to outpace the supply, and thus the body-snatching industry was born. By the early 1700s, it was common for anatomists and their students to engage in a little after-school grave robbing or to employ so-called resurrectionists to exhume the graves of the recently buried (often belonging to the urban poor) in their stead.[29] They were thoroughly despised for it, and public opinion tanked even further when it was revealed that a series of murders had been committed to supply an anatomist in Scotland.[30] Eventually, anatomists were allowed access to the bodies of the workhouse dead with the passing of the 1832 Anatomy Act, though it was really the advent of modern embalming in the late 1800s that brought grave robbing to an end.

Thankfully, there are many (legal) avenues available to us today should you wish to donate your body to science. Dissecting cadavers is a time-honored initiation rite for most aspiring doctors, and medical schools are always in need of new bodies to instruct the next generation of medical students. Donating parts of your body is also an option— as of 2024, more than one hundred thousand people in the United States are on the waiting list for organ transplants, and a new person is added every eight minutes. By signing up to be an organ donor, you have the potential to save up to eight lives.[31] If that doesn't tickle your fancy, you could always join the growing number of Americans offering their bodies up to organizations known as body farms. The first one opened inside the University of Tennessee, Knoxville, in 1987, and it is now possible

Curious Coffins and Riveting Rituals

to donate your body to one of the eight US body farms dedicated to the study of decomposition to aid forensic scientists and detectives in investigating and locating the murdered and missing dead.[32]

Death, as it is meant to happen in nature, always engenders new life. We don't all have the option of leaving our bodies out on mountaintops to give sustenance to giant scavenging birds, but many of us have the option of donating our bodies to causes we care about. And whether your body ends up as a crash test dummy or a practice cadaver on which new medical techniques are tested, opting to have your body (or its parts) donated to those who need it can be a deeply meaningful act. Most body donors remain anonymous, but we owe much of our medical knowledge—and, in some cases, our lives—to the generosity and kindness of those before us.

The . . . End?

Death is, statistically, a thoroughly unremarkable experience. Roughly 60 million people die every year—that's 178,000 people each day, 7,425 per hour, and 120 every minute.[33] Yet when someone we love dies, the resulting grief, anger, and loss may feel so large and endless that it can leave us shattered and disorientated. And so, in these moments of tragedy and change, many of us look to the past. We turn to our rituals of death, as generations of people have done before us.

The world is home to a huge variety of death rituals, some of which we have discussed in this book. Many of them are geographically specific. The Egyptians believed that it was necessary to preserve the entire body for the soul to live on in the afterlife, likely in no small part because they lived in a desert that made the natural desiccation of bodies possible in the first place. The Sioux lived alongside animals more than willing to scavenge human bodies, so they interred their dead on elevated platforms. In the mountains of Tibet, wood is scarce and the ground rocky, so death rituals rarely involve burial or cremation. All over, we see that just as we shape the lands we occupy, so, too, do they shape us. Our ideological and practical concerns are often inextricably interwoven, leading to rituals that can differ significantly from region to region. Many of them have evolved to fit the times, either melding with other ritual beliefs or changing completely in the wake of political reform. Others have been lost forever or are on their way out: threatened by climate change, suppressed by acts of colonial violence, or simply made obsolete by time.

We have not always done well with such diversity of beliefs and practices; the cultural norms that teach us the appropriate ways to inter and memorialize our loved ones are also the same ones that inform our perception of right and wrong. All throughout history, countless have acted on this impulse, mocking others for their beliefs, demonizing what they do not understand, and taking that which does not belong to them. But, of course, there is no right or wrong way to approach death, only cultural variations on the theme. In any case, a world in full agreement would be a monotonous one for sure, and often it is only when you have been exposed to the sheer diversity of ritual experiences that you are truly able to understand and appreciate your own.

But for all our differences, one thing remains the same: From emperors to soldiers to mothers to paupers, we are not only united in our mortality (and our fear of it) but also alike in our grief. History speaks to us in the mottled language of bones, grave goods, and burial mounds, and what it tells us is that we recognize the anguish of the bereaved who lived tens of thousands of years before us, just as they would recognize ours. The same ideas show up in death rituals that develop worlds apart, separated by oceans, geopolitical lines, and religions. Our rituals may look different, or involve different steps, but the message is always the same: I love you. I want you to eat well. I will take care of you—will you take care of me? The dictionary definition of *humanity*, or the quality of being humane, is being sympathetic to and considerate of others—or, in other words, "showing compassion."[34] And that is what our rituals do. We are not born into this world alone, and nor should we leave it alone. Many death rituals are a continuation of existing social relationships, and the Wari' understood that "through our bodies, we are linked to one another, not just by ties of birth and blood, but also by the many forms of sociality and caregiving—the feeding, holding, grooming, cuddling, lovemaking, healing, and work—exchanged in the course of daily life."[35] Caught in this web of obligation, respect, and reciprocation, we ostensibly

Curious Coffins and Riveting Rituals

turn to our rituals to honor and help the dead, but in conducting these ceremonies, we help ourselves, and one another.

Very often, our rituals seem abstract, up until the point where they suddenly aren't. Frank Shyong, a columnist for the *Los Angeles Times*, describes the moment when it all clicked for him in the wake of his grandmother's death: "I light this incense because it's too hard to say goodbye, forever. Sometimes it is easier to say, see you next year. And every year after that."[36] Accepting death doesn't necessarily make saying goodbye any easier, but there will come a time when your rituals make sense, when they will serve as a comfort and a relief, when they become something you need. We may never know for certain what happens after death (or if anything happens at all), but one thing's for sure: We will miss the people we love when they pass on, and they will miss us when it's our turn. And if that sounds like a bittersweet mixed bag of goods . . .

Well, that's life.

Endnotes

Death: A Short Introduction

1   Joseph Campbell and Bill D. Moyers, *The Power of Myth*, ed. Betty Sue Flowers (Turtleback Books, 2012), xi.

2   Anthony F. C. Wallace, *Religion: An Anthropological View* (Random House, 1966), 61.

3   Milton Cohen, "Death Ritual: Anthropological Perspectives," 1, http://www.qcc.cuny.edu/SocialSciences/ppecorino /DeathandDying_TEXT/Death%20Ritual.pdf.

4   Michaeleen Doucleff, "So You Think You Know All About the Plague?," *Goats and Soda* (NPR blog), February 14, 2024, https://www.npr.org/sections/goatsandsoda/2024/02/14 /1231215446/so-you-think-you-know-all-about-the-plague.

5   US Census Bureau, "World War I Casualties," 2011, https://www.census.gov/history/pdf/reperes112018.pdf.

6   More specifically, in 1968, when a committee at Harvard Medical School published a landmark report titled "A Definition of Irreversible Coma," formulating what is now known as brain death.

7   Rob Stein, "Debate Simmers Over When Doctors Should Declare Brain Death," *Shots* (NPR blog), February 11, 2024, https://www.npr.org/sections/health-shots/2024/02/11 /1228330149/brain-death-definition.

8   National Conference of Commissioners on Uniform State Laws, Uniform Determination of Death Act, 2, https://www .uniformlaws.org/viewdocument/final-act-49.

9   Stein, "Debate Simmers Over When Doctors Should Declare Brain Death."

10 Paul Koudounaris, *Memento Mori: The Dead Among Us* (Thames & Hudson, 2015, 18).

11 David San Filippo, "Religious Interpretations of Death, Afterlife & NDEs" (Faculty Publications, National Louis University, January 2006), 7, https://digitalcommons.nl.edu/cgi /viewcontent.cgi?article=1031&context=faculty_publications.

12 Caitlin Doughty, *From Here to Eternity: Traveling the World to Find the Good Death* (W. W. Norton & Company, 2017), 36.

13 James Gire, "How Death Imitates Life: Cultural Influences on Conceptions of Death and Dying," *Online Readings in Psychology and Culture* 6, no. 2 (December 2014): 4, https://doi.org/10.9707/2307-0919.1120.

14 Brian Switek, *Skeleton Keys: The Secret Life of Bone* (Penguin, 2020), 140–41.

15 Pat Lee Shipman, "The Bright Side of the Black Death," *American Scientist*, February 6, 2017, https://www .americanscientist.org/article/the-bright-side-of-the -black-death.

16 Joanna Ebenstein, *Death: A Graveside Companion* (National Geographic Books, 2017), 215–16.

17 Jeremie Zulaski, "Lord of Death, Yogin, Demon: Tracing the Iconographic Symbolism of Yama from the Rig Veda into Tibetan Buddhism" (working paper, University of Wales Trinity Saint David, January 2017), 6–14, https://doi.org /10.13140/RG.2.2.24060.21128.

18 Donald B. Redford, ed., *The Oxford Essential Guide to Egyptian Mythology* (Berkley Books, 2003), 306.

19 Franz Boas, "The Origin of Death," *Journal of American Folklore* 30, no. 118 (1917): 486, https://doi.org/10.2307/534498.

20 *Merriam-Webster Dictionary*, "superstition," accessed September 9, 2024, https://www.merriam-webster.com/dictionary /superstition.

21 Richard Webster, *The Encyclopedia of Superstitions* (Llewellyn Worldwide, 2012), 182.

22 Madeline Diamond, "20 Bizarre Superstitions from Around the World and the Meaning Behind Them," *Business Insider*, September 27, 2018, https://www.businessinsider.com /superstitions-around-the-world-2017-9#japan-tucking-in -your-thumbs-in-a-cemetery-9.

23 Izzo, Jack. "Did Mass Cat Killings Help Spread the Black Death in the Middle Ages?" Snopes, November 8, 2023. https://www.snopes.com/news/2023/11/08/cats-mass -killings-plague/.

24 Elizabeth Yuko, "Why Black Cats Are Associated with Halloween and Bad Luck," History, October 13, 2021, https://www.history.com/news/black-cats-superstitions.

25 Colin Dickey, "Behind the Draped Mirror," *Hazlitt*, September 28, 2015, https://hazlitt.net/feature/behind-draped-mirror; and Aaron Homer, "The Cultural Significance of Covering Mirrors After Death," *Grunge*, July 21, 2022, https://www .grunge.com/936219/the-cultural-significance-of-covering -mirrors-after-death/.

26 Webster, *Encyclopedia of Superstitions*, 40.

Dead: What Happens to Our Bodies When We Die?

1   Philip Lieberman, *Uniquely Human: The Evolution of Speech, Thought, and Selfless Behavior* (Harvard University Press, 1991), 162–63.

2   More specifically, bones were dated to be from fifty thousand to fifty-eight thousand years ago. See Lorna Tilley, "Care Among the Neandertals: La Chapelle-aux-Saints 1 and La Ferrassie 1 (Case Study 2)," in *Theory and Practice in the Bioarchaeology of Care* (Springer, 2015): 219–57, https://link.springer.com/chapter/10.1007/978-3-319 -18860-7_9.

3   Brian Switek, *Skeleton Keys: The Secret Life of Bone* (Penguin, 2020), 139–40.

4   Qian Sun and Xuguo Zhou, "Corpse Management in Social Insects," *International Journal of Biological Sciences* 9, no. 3 (March 2013): 313–21, https://www.ijbs.com/v09p0313.htm.

5   "Kenya Elephant Buries Its Victims," *BBC News*, last
     updated June 18, 2004, http://news.bbc.co.uk/2/hi
     /africa/3818833.stm.

6   Greg Melville, *Over My Dead Body: Unearthing the Hidden
     History of America's Cemeteries* (Abrams Press, 2022), 13.

7   Including, but not limited to, using razors to slice the soles
     of the feet, jamming needles under toenails, pinching nip-
     ples, and thrusting a red-hot poker up "the rear passage."
     See Mary Roach, *Stiff: The Curious Lives of Human Cadavers*
     (W. W. Norton & Company, 2003), 171.

8   Joshua Foer, Ella Morton, and Dylan Thuras, *Atlas Obscura:
     An Explorer's Guide to the World's Hidden Wonders*, 2nd ed.
     (Workman Publishing Company, 2019), 392.

9   Melville, *Over My Dead Body*, 2.

10   Caitlin Doughty, *From Here to Eternity: Traveling the World to
     Find the Good Death* (W. W. Norton & Company, 2017), 145.

11   "Manage the Burial," MyLegacy@LifeSG, accessed Janu-
     ary 28, 2022, https://mylegacy.life.gov.sg/when-death
     -happens/manage-the-burial/.

12   Sally Hayden, "Ghanaian Funerals: Themed Coffins and
     Dancing Pallbearers," *Irish Times*, May 17, 2022.

13   Kristin Otto, "Shapes of the Ancestors: Bodies, Animals,
     Art, and Ghanaian Fantasy Coffins," *Museum Anthropology
     Review* 13, no. 1–2 (March 2019): 49, https://doi.org/10.14434
     /mar.v13i1.26580.

14   Regula Tschumi and Michael Foster, "The Figurative Palan-
     quins of the Ga: History and Significance." *African Arts* 46,
     no. 4 (Winter 2013): 60.

15   Tschumi and Foster, "The Figurative Palanquins of the Ga,"
     62–67.

16   Hayden, "Ghanaian Funerals."

17   Dennis B. Batangan et al., *The Road to Empowerment:
     Strengthening the Indigenous Peoples Rights Act*, ed. Yasmin
     D. Arquiza, vol. 2, *Nurturing the Earth, Nurturing Life* (Interna-
     tional Labour Organization, 2007), 4, https://www.ilo.org/sites
     /default/files/wcmsp5/groups/public/@asia/@ro-bangkok
     /@ilo-manila/documents/publication/wcms_124793.pdf.

18   Foer, Morton, and Thuras, *Atlas Obscura*, 177.

19   Asia Featured, "The Hanging Coffins of Sagada," streamed
     on April 26, 2020, YouTube video, 3:46, https://www.youtube
     .com/watch?v=myEFOgmE1VI&ab_channel=AsiaFeatured.

20   Richard Collett, "Dark Tourism: The Hanging Coffins of
     Sagada," Travel Tramp, November 8, 2019, https://www
     .travel-tramp.com/hanging-coffins-of-sagada-philippines/.

21   Collett, "Dark Tourism."

22   Ella Cara Deloria, *The Dakota Way of Life* (University of
     Nebraska Press, 2022), 163–65.

23   Melville, *Over My Dead Body*, 30.

24   Melville, 31.

25   Logan Jaffe, "Remains of Thousands of Native Americans
     Were Returned in 2023," *ProPublica*, December 26, 2023,
     https://www.propublica.org/article/repatriation-progress
     -in-2023.

26   "US Indian Boarding School History," National Native Amer-
     ican Boarding School Healing Coalition, February 13, 2018,
     https://boardingschoolhealing.org/education/us-indian
     -boarding-school-history/.

27   Associated Press, "U.S. Report Identifies Burial Sites Linked
     to Boarding Schools for Native Americans," NPR, May 11,
     2022, https://www.npr.org/2022/05/11/1098276649/u-s
     -report-details-burial-sites-linked-to-boarding-schools
     -for-native-americans.

28   Erin Blakemore, "A Century of Trauma at U.S. Boarding
     Schools for Native American Children," *National Geographic*,
     July 9, 2021, https://www.nationalgeographic.com/history
     /article/a-century-of-trauma-at-boarding-schools-for
     -native-american-children-in-the-united-states.

29   James Stevens Curl, *A Celebration of Death: An Introduction
     to Some of the Buildings, Monuments, and Settings of Funerary
     Architecture in the Western European Tradition* (Constable &
     Co., 1980), 25.

30   Leo Benedictus, "Where in the World Is It Illegal to Die?,"
     Guardian, September 30, 2015, https://www.theguardian.com
     /cities/2015/sep/30/where-in-the-world-is-it-illegal-to-die.

31   Francois Pieter Retief and Louise Cilliers, "Burial Customs,
     the Afterlife and the Pollution of Death in Ancient Greece,"
     Acta Theologica 26, no. 2 (March 2006), 44–61, https://doi.org
     /10.4314/actat.v26i2.52560.

32   Retief and Cilliers, "Burial Customs," 44.

33   Retief and Cilliers, 53–55.

34   Department of Greek and Roman Art, "Death, Burial, and
     the Afterlife in Ancient Greece," Metropolitan Museum of
     Art, October 2003, https://www.metmuseum.org/toah/hd
     /dbag/hd_dbag.htm.

35   Radcliffe G. Edmonds III, "Underworld," *Oxford Classical
     Dictionary* (online), April 26, 2019, https://doi.org/10.1093
     /acrefore/9780199381135.013.8062.

36   "Cultural Objects Names Authority Iconography Display,"
     accessed June 30, 2024, http://vocab.getty.edu/page/ia
     /901000317.

37   "Religious Composition by Country, 2010–2050," Pew
     Research Center, December 21, 2022, https://www
     .pewresearch.org/religion/interactives/religious-composition
     -by-country-2010-2050/.

38   Including Roman Catholicism, Protestantism, and Eastern
     Orthodoxy, just to name a few.

39   1 Corinthians 6:19.

40   Romans 8:23; 1 Corinthians 15:52–53; and Revelation 21:4–5,
     22:1–5.

41   Raymond Angelo Belliotti, *Dante's Deadly Sins: Moral Philoso-
     phy in Hell* (Wiley–Blackwell, 2011), 23–46.

42   Douglas O. Linder, "Questions & Answers Concerning Indul-
     gences," UMKC School of Law, accessed September 9, 2024,
     https://famous-trials.com/luther/295-indulgences.

43   Jon G. Hughes with Sophie Gallagher, *Witches, Druids, and
     Sin Eaters: The Common Magic of the Cunning Folk of the Welsh
     Marches* (Destiny Books, 2022), 242–44.

44   "Religious Composition by Country, 2010–2050."

45   A. R. Gatrad, "Muslim Customs Surrounding Death, Bereave-ment, Postmortem Examinations, and Organ Transplants," *BMJ* 309, no. 6953 (August 1994): 521, https://doi.org/10.1136/bmj.309.6953.521.

46   Jack Hartnell, *Medieval Bodies: Life, Death and Art in the Middle Ages* (Profile Books, 2018), 118.

47   Melville, *Over My Dead Body*, 18.

48   Melville, 18.

49   "Mausoleum of the First Qin Emperor," UNESCO World Heri-tage Convention, accessed September 9, 2024, https://whc.unesco.org/en/list/441/.

50   Zhixin Jason Sun, *Age of Empires: Art of the Qin and Han Dynas-ties* (Metropolitan Museum of Art, 2017), 80–82.

51   Elizabeth Quill, "Were the Terracotta Warriors Based on Actual People?," *Smithsonian*, March 2015, https://www.smithsonianmag.com/history/were-terracotta-warriors-based-on-actual-people-180954321/.

52   Melville, *Over My Dead Body*, 17.

53   John Roach, "Emperor Qin's Tomb," *National Geographic*, October 9, 2009, https://www.nationalgeographic.com/history/article/emperor-qin.

54   See the stone warriors of Shizishan, Xuzhou, at the Xuzhou Museum, https://www.xzmuseum.com/ecollection_detail.aspx?id=19467.

55   "The Viking Age," National Museum of Denmark, 2015, https://en.natmus.dk/historical-knowledge/denmark/prehistoric-period-until-1050-ad/the-viking-age/.

56   Stefan Brink and Neil Price, eds., *The Viking World* (Routledge, 2011), 261.

57   Thomas A. DuBois, *Nordic Religions in the Viking Age* (Univer-sity of Pennsylvania Press, 1999), 79–80.

58   Brink and Price, *Viking World*, 258–59.

59   As seen with Rakni's Mound.

60   Hilda E. Davidson, "Valkyries," in *Medieval Folklore: An Ency-clopedia of Myths, Legends, Tales, Beliefs, and Customs*, ed. Carl Lindahl (ABC-CLIO, 2000), 1014–15.

61   Brink and Price, *Viking World*, 266.

62   Thorleif Sjøvold, *The Oseberg Find and the Other Viking Ship Finds* (Universitetets Oldsaksamling, 1963), 10.

63   Sjøvold, *Oseberg Find*, 32.

64   DuBois, *Nordic Religions*, 73–74.

65   "Bucket of yew wooden, with brass and iron decora-tion. Inside they found a wooden ladle and 6 or 7 wild apples. Found in the Tomb of the Oseberg Ship. 9th century. Viking Ship Museum. Oslo. Norway," Alamy, accessed January 8, 2025, https://www.alamy.com/bucket-of-yew-wooden-with-brass-and-iron-decoration-inside-they-found-a-wooden-ladle-and-6-or-7-wild-apples-found-in-the-tomb-of-the-oseberg-ship-9th-century-viking-ship-museum-oslo-norway-image231217228.html.

66   "The Collection," Museum of the Viking Age, accessed January 8, 2025, https://www.vikingtidsmuseet.no/english/the-collection.

67   Nina Kristiansen, "This bucket remained buried in a Viking grave for 1,000 years, but is in excellent condition," ScienceNorway.no, January 12, 2024, accessed January 8, 2025, https://www.sciencenorway.no/archaeology-history-viking-age/this-bucket-remained-buried-in-a-viking-grave-for-1000-years-but-is-in-excellent-condition/2308233.

68   Loren Rhoads, *199 Cemeteries to See Before You Die* (Running Press, 2017), 152.

69   "Our Story," Green-Wood, 2011, https://www.green-wood.com/about-history/.

70   Melville, *Over My Dead Body*, 63–64.

71   Rhoads, *199 Cemeteries*, 159.

72   "Okunoin Temple," Japan Guide, 2023, https://www.japan-guide.com/e/e4901.html.

73   J. E. Cirlot, *A Dictionary of Symbols* (Courier Corporation, 2013), 105.

74   "Mungo Lady," National Museum of Australia, updated Sep-tember 28, 2022, https://www.nma.gov.au/defining-moments/resources/mungo-lady.

75   Doughty, *From Here to Eternity*, 20.

76   Melville, *Over My Dead Body*, 194.

77   Melville, 195.

78   Roach, *Stiff*, 259.

79   Melville, *Over My Dead Body*, 195.

80   Melville, 199.

81   The Wise Apple, "The Ecological Benefits of Fire," *National Geographic*, last updated August 15, 2024, https://education.nationalgeographic.org/resource/ecological-benefits-fire/.

82   Hindu cremations are traditionally conducted and attended by men, but nowhere in the Hindu scriptures does it say that women should be banned from witnessing and participat-ing in these last rites. Many women have since begun to push back against this outmoded idea. See Geeta Pandey, "Mandira Bedi: What Hindu Scriptures Say About Women at Cremations," *BBC News*, July 20, 2021, https://www.bbc.com/news/world-asia-india-57894855.

83   David Arnold, *Burning the Dead: Hindu Nationhood and the Global Construction of Indian Tradition* (University of California Press, 2021), 8.

84   Doughty, *From Here to Eternity*, 36–37.

85   Pete McBride, "The Pyres of Varanasi: Breaking the Cycle of Death and Rebirth," *National Geographic*, August 7, 2014, https://www.nationalgeographic.com/photography/article/the-pyres-of-varanasi-breaking-the-cycle-of-death-and-rebirth.

86   James Pasley, "Inside Varanasi, India's Holy 'City of Death,' Where People Hoping to Break the Hindu Cycle of Rebirth Go to Die," *Business Insider*, June 2, 2023, https://www.businessinsider.com/photos-varanasi-india-city-of-death-tourism-2023-6.

87   Doughty, *From Here to Eternity*, 29.

88   Sreya Panuganti, "Come Hell or Holy Water," *Corporate Knights* 16, no. 3 (Summer 2017): 51, https://www.jstor.org/stable/26789209.

89 Oliver Franklin-Wallis, "Inside India's Gargantuan Mission to Clean the Ganges River," *Wired*, November 30, 2023, https://www.wired.com/story/india-ganges-river-clean-project/.

90 Andrew Bernstein, "Fire and Earth: The Forging of Modern Cremation in Meiji Japan," *Japanese Journal of Religious Studies* 27, no. 3/4 (Fall 2000): 297–98, http://www.jstor.org/stable/30233668.

91 Anna Hiatt, "The History of Cremation in Japan," *JSTOR Daily*, September 9, 2015, https://daily.jstor.org/history-japan-cremation/.

92 Bernstein, "Fire and Earth," 298.

93 Bernstein, 298.

94 Motoko Rich, "Crematory Is Booked? Japan Offers Corpse Hotels," *The New York Times*, July 1, 2017, https://www.nytimes.com/2017/07/01/world/asia/japan-corpse-hotels.html.

95 Leo Lewis, "Corpse Hotels Cater to Japan's Waiting Dead," *Financial Times*, November 7, 2018, https://www.ft.com/content/99e43d70-e1b2-11e8-8e70-5e22a430c1ad.

96 Doughty, *From Here to Eternity*, 169–70.

97 James Gire, "How Death Imitates Life: Cultural Influences on Conceptions of Death and Dying," *Online Readings in Psychology and Culture* 6, no. 2 (December 2014): 9–10, https://doi.org/10.9707/2307-0919.1120.

98 Gire, "How Death Imitates Life," 9–10.

99 The Mainichi Newspapers. "Nearly Half Say Maintaining Graves Is Hard Work: Japan Firm's Survey." *The Mainichi*, September 24, 2024. https://mainichi.jp/english/articles/20240921/p2a/00m/0na/018000c.

100 Doughty, *From Here to Eternity*, 186.

101 Melville, *Over My Dead Body*, 195–96.

102 Caitlin Doughty, "What Happens to a Body During Cremation?," streamed on April 13, 2018, YouTube video, 6:42, https://www.youtube.com/watch?v=6TSFX-hFglk&ab_channel=CaitlinDoughty.

103 Joseph Campbell and Bill D. Moyers, *The Power of Myth*, ed. Betty Sue Flowers (Turtleback Books, 2012), 218.

104 In any case, there are reasons why we haven't evolved to farm and eat our own, one of them being that we aren't very nutritious—and definitely not worth the trouble of hunting down and cooking.

105 Josh Davis, "Oldest Evidence of Human Cannibalism as a Funerary Practice," Natural History Museum, October 4, 2023, https://www.nhm.ac.uk/discover/news/2023/october/oldest-evidence-of-human-cannibalism-as-a-funerary-practice.html.

106 Lisa Hendry, "The Cannibals of Gough's Cave," Natural History Museum, December 19, 2017, https://www.nhm.ac.uk/discover/the-cannibals-of-goughs-cave.html.

107 Davis, "Oldest Evidence of Human Cannibalism as a Funerary Practice."

108 Ben Thomas, "Eating People Is Wrong—but It's Also Widespread and Sacred," *Sapiens*, April 20, 2017, https://www.sapiens.org/biology/cannibalism-ritualized-sacred/.

109 Abby Riehl, "'The Bread of Life': Exploring Ritualistic Cannibalism," *Epoch*, September 2020, https://www.epoch-magazine.com/riehlthebreadoflife.

110 P. Kenneth Himmelman, "The Medicinal Body: An Analysis of Medicinal Cannibalism in Europe, 1300–1700," *Dialectical Anthropology* 22, no. 2 (June 1997): 197, http://www.jstor.org/stable/29790453.

111 The practice was first documented around the Tang dynasty (618–907 CE), growing so popular that by the sixteenth and seventeenth centuries, it had become a culturally established gesture of filial devotion. See Jimmy Yu, *Sanctity and Self-Inflicted Violence in Chinese Religions, 1500–1700* (Oxford University Press, 2012), https://doi.org/10.1093/acprof:oso/9780199844906.001.0001.

112 Beth A. Conklin, *Consuming Grief: Compassionate Cannibalism in an Amazonian Society* (University of Texas Press, 2001), 4.

113 Caitlin Doughty, *Smoke Gets in Your Eyes: And Other Lessons from the Crematory* (W. W. Norton & Company, 2014), 67–68.

114 Thomas, "Eating People Is Wrong."

115 Conklin, *Consuming Grief*, xvi–xvii.

116 Doughty, *Smoke Gets in Your Eyes*, 69.

117 Conklin, *Consuming Grief*, xvii–xviii.

118 Conklin, xix–xxi.

119 Conklin, xvii–xviii.

120 Conklin, xix.

121 Doughty, *Smoke Gets in Your Eyes*, 82.

122 Sangye Khadro, *Preparing for Death and Helping the Dying: A Buddhist Perspective* (Kong Meng San Phor Kark See Monastery, 1999; repr., 2005), 23. The page citation refers to the reprint.

123 Doughty, *Smoke Gets in Your Eyes*, 224–225.

124 Jivanji Jamshedji Modi, *The Funeral Ceremonies of the Parsees: Their Origin and Explanation*, 4th ed. (Fort Printing Press, 1928), https://www.avesta.org/ritual/funeral.htm.

125 Bachi Karkaria, "Death in the City: How a Lack of Vultures Threatens Mumbai's 'Towers of Silence,'" *Guardian*, January 26, 2015, https://www.theguardian.com/cities/2015/jan/26/death-city-lack-vultures-threatens-mumbai-towers-of-silence.

126 Karkaria, "Death in the City."

127 Karkaria, "Death in the City."

128 Karkaria, "Death in the City."

129 Doughty, *Smoke Gets in Your Eyes*, 222.

130 Elliot Hannon, "Vanishing Vultures a Grave Matter for India's Parsis," NPR, September 5, 2012, https://www.npr.org/2012/09/05/160401322/vanishing-vultures-a-grave-matter-for-indias-parsis.

131 "Disposition Statistics for Media," Green Burial Council, December 29, 2023, https://www.greenburialcouncil.org/disposition-statistics-media.html.

132 "Disposition Statistics for Media."

133 Michael J. Coren, "Comparing Green Funeral Options, from Composting to Natural Burial to Water Cremation," *Washington Post*, January 31, 2023,

https://www.washingtonpost.com/climate
-environment/2023/01/31/green-funeral-options
-cremation-burial/.

134 Roach, *Stiff*, 261–62.

135 Roach, 264–65.

136 Nora McGreevy, "What Did Tollund Man, One of Europe's Famed Bog Bodies, Eat Before He Died?," *Smithsonian*, July 22, 2021, https://www.smithsonianmag.com/smart -news/tollund-man-europe-bog-body-meal-food-history -mummy-180978247/.

137 Elise Cutts, "These Mummies Were Made . . . by Accident?," *National Geographic*, August 7, 2023, https://www .nationalgeographic.com/science/article/natural -mummies-accident.

138 Cutts, "These Mummies Were Made."

139 National Geographic Staff, "Frozen Inca Mummy Goes on Display," *National Geographic*, September 11, 2007, https:// www.nationalgeographic.com/science/article/news-inca -argentina-la-doncella-sacrifice-archaeology.

140 McGreevy, "What Did Tollund Man, One of Europe's Famed Bog Bodies, Eat Before He Died?"

141 Erich Brenner, "Human Body Preservation—Old and New Techniques," *Journal of Anatomy* 224, no. 3 (March 2014): 316–44, https://doi.org/10.1111/joa.12160.

142 Juan Francisco Riumalló, "The Ancient Mummies Older than Egypt's," *BBC Travel*, May 20, 2022, https://www.bbc.com /travel/article/20220519-chiles-desert-town-built-on -mummies.

143 Doughty, *From Here to Eternity*, 85.

144 Nicholas St. Fleur, "How to Make a Mummy (Accidentally)," *The New York Times*, June 2, 2017, https://www.nytimes.com /2017/06/02/science/spontaneous-mummification.html.

145 Hartnell, *Medieval Bodies*, 47.

146 David Farley, "The Bone Collectors," *Slate*, October 20, 2009, https://slate.com/human-interest/2009/10/it-s-time-to-bring -relics-back-to-the-catholic-church.html.

147 Charles Freeman, *Holy Bones, Holy Dust: How Relics Shaped the History of Medieval Europe* (Yale University Press, 2011), xiii-xiv.

148 Hartnell, *Medieval Bodies*, 175.

149 Switek, *Skeleton Keys*, 144.

150 Hartnell, *Medieval Bodies*, 49–50.

151 "Tomb of St. Catherine of Siena," Basilica Santa Maria Sopra Minerva, April 15, 2019, https://www.santamaria -sopraminerva.it/en/5-tomb-of-st-catherine-of-siena.html.

152 "Facing the Past: The Jericho Skull," British Museum (web-site), January 17, 2017, https://www.britishmuseum.org/blog /facing-past-jericho-skull.

153 Jennifer Billock, "This Austrian Ossuary Holds Hundreds of Elaborately Hand-Painted Skulls," *Smithsonian*, September 15, 2017, https://www.smithsonianmag.com/travel/hallstatt -bones-house-hand-painted-skulls-180964736/.

154 Doughty, *From Here to Eternity*, 190.

155 Doughty, 191.

156 Referring to the Indigenous societies of the Andes, partic-ularly those who came under the rule or influence of the Incan Empire, which stretched across Chile, Peru, Bolivia, Colombia, and Ecuador.

157 Christine Bednarz, "See Bolivia's Celebration of Human Skulls," *National Geographic*, December 17, 2018, https://www .nationalgeographic.com/travel/article/la-paz-natitas -things-to-do-skull-festival-cemetery.

158 Rachel Nuwer, "Meet the Celebrity Skulls of Bolivia's Fiesta de Las Ñatitas," *Smithsonian*, November 17, 2015, https://www.smithsonianmag.com/arts-culture/meet -celebrity-skulls-bolivias-fiesta-de-las-natitas-180957289/.

159 Bednarz, "See Bolivia's Celebration of Human Skulls."

160 Nuwer, "Meet the Celebrity Skulls of Bolivia's Fiesta de Las Ñatitas."

161 Nuwer, "Meet the Celebrity Skulls of Bolivia's Fiesta de Las Ñatitas."

162 Koudounaris, *Memento Mori*, 159–160.

163 "Egyptian Mummies," Smithsonian Institution, October 8, 2017, https://www.si.edu/spotlight/ancient-egypt/mummies.

164 Cats, for example, were linked to the goddess Bastet, hawks to Horus, and Apis bulls to Osiris. See "Egyp-tian Animals Were Mummified Same Way as Humans," *National Geographic*, September 15, 2004, https:// www.nationalgeographic.com/science/article /news-egyptian-animals-mummies-archaeology.

165 "Egyptian Mummies."

166 A golden age in Egypt encompassing the eighteenth, nineteenth, and twentieth dynasties, stretching from the sixteenth century to eleventh century BCE.

167 "Canopic Jar," 664–525 BCE, limestone and paint, 11 x 6 ⅛ in., Metropolitan Museum of Art, New York, object no. 12.183.1a.1, .2, https://www.metmuseum.org/art/collection /search/550773.

168 Francesco Carelli, "The Book of Death: Weighing Your Heart," *London Journal of Primary Care* 4, no. 1 (July 2011): 87–88, https://doi.org/10.1080/17571472.2011.11493336.

169 Bill Schutt, *Cannibalism: A Perfectly Natural History* (Algonquin Books, 2018), 216.

170 Roach, *Stiff*, 223.

171 Mariel Carr, "Mummies and the Usefulness of Death," Sci-ence History Institute Museum & Library, October 13, 2014, accessed January 8, 2025, https://www.sciencehistory.org /stories/magazine/mummies-and-the-usefulness-of-death/.

172 Anita Pisch, "The Phenomenon of the Personality Cult—a Historical Perspective," in *The Personality Cult of Stalin in Soviet Posters, 1929–1953: Archetypes, Inventions and Fabrications* (ANU Press, 2016), 53, http://www.jstor.org /stable/j.ctt1q1crzp.7.

173 Pisch, "The Phenomenon of the Personality Cult," 55.

174 Robert C. Tucker, "The Rise of Stalin's Personality Cult," *American Historical Review* 84, no. 2 (April 1979): 347, https://doi.org/10.2307/1855137.

175 Daria Litvinova, "Lenin Lab: The Team Keeping the First Soviet Leader Embalmed," *Guardian*, May 9, 2016, https://www.theguardian.com/world/2016/may/09/lenin-lab-team-keeping-first-soviet-leader-embalmed-moscow.

176 "Preserving Chairman Mao: Embalming a Body to Maintain a Legacy," *Guardian*, September 11, 2016, https://www.theguardian.com/world/2016/sep/11/preserving-chairman-mao-embalming-a-body-to-maintain-a-legacy.

177 Marianka Swain, "The Strange, Grisly Saga of Eva Perón's Corpse," *Telegraph*, July 25, 2022, https://www.telegraph.co.uk/tv/0/strange-grisly-saga-eva-Peróns-corpse/.

178 Linda Pressly, "The 20-Year Odyssey of Eva Perón's Body," *BBC News*, June 26, 2012, https://www.bbc.com/news/magazine-18616380.

179 He served as president of Argentina for the first time from 1946 to 1952, again from 1952 to 1955, and finally from 1973 until his death in 1974.

180 Alexander Craig, "Perón and Peronism: Personalism Personified," *International Journal* 31, no. 4 (Autumn 1976): 708, https://doi.org/10.2307/40201381.

181 Koudounaris, *Memento Mori*, 131.

182 "The Capuchin Catacombs," Palermo Catacombs (website), September 10, 2014, https://www.palermocatacombs.com/.

183 Foer, Morton, and Thuras, *Atlas Obscura*, 60.

184 Foer, Morton, and Thuras, 60.

185 "The Capuchin Catacombs."

186 Doughty, *From Here to Eternity*, 45.

187 Hayley Campbell, *All the Living and the Dead: A Personal Investigation into the Death Trade* (Raven Books, 2022), 139.

188 Doughty, *From Here to Eternity*, 74–75.

189 Doughty, 50.

190 Anastasia Baan, Markus Deli Girik Allo, and Andi Anto Patak, "The Cultural Attitudes of a Funeral Ritual Discourse in the Indigenous Torajan, Indonesia," *Heliyon* 8, no. 2 (February 2022), https://doi.org/10.1016/j.heliyon.2022.e08925.

191 Foer, Morton, and Thuras, *Atlas Obscura*, 166.

192 Foer, Morton, and Thuras, 166.

193 Koudounaris, *Memento Mori*, 18.

194 Ken Jeremiah, *Living Buddhas: The Self-Mummified Monks of Yamagata, Japan* (McFarland, 2014), 11.

195 Jeremiah, *Living Buddhas*, 11.

196 Jeremiah, 12.

197 Foer, Morton, and Thuras, *Atlas Obscura*, 157.

198 Jeremiah, *Living Buddhas*, 12.

199 Jeremiah, 12.

200 Foer, Morton, and Thuras, *Atlas Obscura*, 157.

201 Melville, *Over My Dead Body*, 127.

202 Michael Washburn, "Decomposure," *UChicago Magazine*, March–April 2013, https://mag.uchicago.edu/law-policy-society/decomposure#.

203 Melville, *Over My Dead Body*, 118.

204 Campbell, *All the Living and the Dead*, 124–25.

205 Campbell, 124.

206 Melville, *Over My Dead Body*, 124.

207 Campbell, *All the Living and the Dead*, 125.

208 Doughty, 74.

Very Dead: How Do We Remember Our Dead?

1 Full quote: "Someday soon, perhaps in forty years, there will be no one alive who has ever known me. That's when I will be truly dead—when I exist in no one's memory. I thought a lot about how someone very old is the last living individual to have known some person or cluster of people. When that person dies, the whole cluster dies, too, vanishes from the living memory. I wonder who that person will be for me. Whose death will make me truly dead?"

2 Nigel Barley, *Grave Matters: A Lively History of Death Around the World* (Henry Holt & Co., 1997), 29.

3 Linda Sun Crowder, "Chinese Funerals in San Francisco Chinatown: American Chinese Expressions in Mortuary Ritual Performance," *Journal of American Folklore* 113, no. 450 (2000): 452, https://doi.org/10.2307/542042.

4 Harry Garlick, *The Final Curtain: State Funerals and the Theatre of Power* (Brill Rodopi, 1999), 1.

5 "State Funerals: United States of America," JTF-NCR/USAMDW, February 15, 2013, https://usstatefuneral.mdw.army.mil/.

6 Aaron Brown, "Funeral of Sir Winston Churchill: 50 Years Since Britain Buried Its Iconic Wartime Leader," *Express*, January 30, 2015, https://www.express.co.uk/news/history/554733/Sir-Winston-Churchill-State-Funeral-50-Anniversary-Wartime-Prime-Minister.

7 Joseph Campbell and Bill D. Moyers, *The Power of Myth*, ed. Betty Sue Flowers (Turtleback Books, 2012), xii.

8 Lisa Levy, "Women's Expressions of Grief, from Mourning Clothes to Memory Books," *JSTOR Daily*, December 10, 2014, https://daily.jstor.org/women-and-mourning/.

9 "Mourning—Indigenous Australia," Australian Museum, updated November 22, 2018, https://australian.museum/about/history/exhibitions/death-the-last-taboo/mourning-indigenous-australia/.

10 "Mourning Fashion," William L. Clements Library, July 22, 2019, https://clements.umich.edu/exhibit/death-in-early-america/mourning-fashion/.

11 Bernard Edem Dzramedo, Robert Ahiabor, and Richard Gbadegbe, "The Relevance and Symbolism of Clothes Within Traditional Institutions and Its Modern Impacts on the Ghanaian Culture," *Arts and Design Studies* 13 (2013): 9, https://www.iiste.org/Journals/index.php/ADS/article/view/8079.

12 Lee Kwang Kyu, "The Concept of Ancestors and Ancestor Worship in Korea," *Asian Folklore Studies* 43, no. 2 (1984): 202–3, https://doi.org/10.2307/1178009.

13   Demetrios Protopsaltis, *An Encyclopedic Chronology of Greece and Its History* (Xlibris Corporation, 2012), 142.

14   "Jewish Graves: Stones of Remembrance," Beth El Mausoleum, June 7, 2022, https://bethelmausoleum.org/2022/06/07/jewish-graves-stones-of-remembrance/.

15   Erin Blakemore, "Why Women Bring Their 'I Voted' Stickers to Susan B. Anthony's Grave," *Smithsonian*, updated October 28, 2020, https://www.smithsonianmag.com/smart-news/why-women-bring-their-i-voted-stickers-susan-b-anthonys-grave-180958847/.

16   KTRK-TV, "What Do Coins on Military Tombstones Mean?," ABC 7 Chicago, May 28, 2017, https://abc7chicago.com/memorial-day-coins-on-tombstone-tombstones-fallen-soldiers/2048071/.

17   "Why We Wear Poppies on Remembrance Day," Imperial War Museums, October 31, 2014, https://www.iwm.org.uk/history/why-we-wear-poppies-on-remembrance-day.

18   Jessica Roux, *Floriography: An Illustrated Guide to the Victorian Language of Flowers* (Andrews McMeel Publishing, 2020), 40–42.

19   Gretchen Scoble and Ann Field, *The Meaning of Flowers: Myth, Language & Lore* (Chronicle Books, 2014), 6.

20   Roux, *Floriography*, 133–35.

21   Vanessa Romo, "Why Marigolds, or Cempasúchil, Are the Iconic Flower of Día de Los Muertos," NPR, October 30, 2021, https://www.npr.org/2021/10/30/1050726374/why-marigolds-or-cempasuchil-are-the-iconic-flower-of-dia-de-los-muertos.

22   Amy McKeever, "How the Soulful Marigold Became an Icon, from Mexico to India," *National Geographic*, October 24, 2022, https://www.nationalgeographic.com/history/article/how-the-marigold-became-a-global-icon-from-mexico-to-india.

23   Joanna Ebenstein, *Death: A Graveside Companion* (Thames & Hudson, 2017), 337; and Caroline Walker Bynum and Paula Gerson, "Body-Part Reliquaries and Body Parts in the Middle Ages," *Gesta* 36, no. 1 (1997): 3–7, https://www.jstor.org/stable/767274.

24   Ebenstein, *Death*, 84. This section was written by Karen Bachmann, a master jewelry model maker and adjunct professor at the Pratt Institute.

25   Marilyn A. Mendoza, "Death and Bereavement Among the Lakota," *Psychology Today*, October 7, 2017, https://www.psychologytoday.com/us/blog/understanding-grief/201710/death-and-bereavement-among-the-lakota.

26   Eve A. Hargrave et al., eds., *Transforming the Dead: Culturally Modified Bone in the Prehistoric Midwest* (University of Alabama Press, 2015), 256.

27   Jo Munnik and Katy Scott, "In Famadihana, Madagascar, a Sacred Ritual Unearths the Dead," CNN, updated March 27, 2017, https://www.cnn.com/2016/10/18/travel/madagascar-turning-bones/index.html.

28   Munnik and Scott, "In Famadihana, Madagascar, a Sacred Ritual Unearths the Dead."

29   Munnik and Scott, "In Famadihana, Madagascar, a Sacred Ritual Unearths the Dead."

30   Dan Waters, "Chinese Funerals: A Case Study," *Journal of the Hong Kong Branch of the Royal Asiatic Society* 31 (1991), 129–30, https://www.jstor.org/stable/23891029.

31   "Chinese Mythology: Da Shi Ye, the King of Hell," Xiao En, August 19, 2021, https://xiao-en.com/chinese-mythology-da-shi-ye-the-king-of-hell/.

32   Cheryl Sim, "Zhong Yuan Jie (Hungry Ghost Festival)," National Library Board Singapore, accessed September 10, 2024, https://www.nlb.gov.sg/main/article-detail?cmsuuid=fe14c69f-7d05-4844-abae-de842064f5ce.

33   Oscar Lopez, "What Is Day of the Dead, the Mexican Holiday?," *The New York Times*, October 31, 2023, https://www.nytimes.com/article/day-of-the-dead-mexico.html.

34   Ebenstein, *Death*, 214–15. This section is by Eva Aridjis, a Mexican filmmaker and lecturer.

35   Caitlin Doughty, *From Here to Eternity: Traveling the World to Find the Good Death* (W. W. Norton & Company, 2017), 94.

36   Ebenstein, *Death*, 214.

37   Doughty, *From Here to Eternity*, 84.

38   Chelsea Hylton, "The Meanings Behind the Items on the Día de Muertos Ofrenda," *Los Angeles Times*, October 25, 2023, https://www.latimes.com/delos/story/2023-10-25/ofrenda-altar-dia-de-muertos.

39   Liu, "Ancestral Altars."

40   Crowder, "Chinese Funerals in San Francisco Chinatown," 452.

41   "Treasures: Tusk," National Museum of African Art, 2008, https://africa.si.edu/exhibits/treasures2008/tusk3.html.

42   "The Kingdom of Benin," National Museum of African Art.

43   "Benin Bronzes," British Museum, July 2, 2021, https://www.britishmuseum.org/about-us/british-museum-story/contested-objects-collection/benin-bronzes.

44   Benin artist, "Rattle Staff," 1900s, wood and cowrie shells, 58 7/8 x 2 15/16 x 3 1/8, Cleveland Museum of Art, Cleveland, object no. 1998.85, https://www.clevelandart.org/art/1998.85.

45   Benin artist, "Head of an Oba," 19th century, brass and iron, 13 1/4 x 10 3/4 x 11 1/8 in., Metropolitan Museum of Art, New York, object no. 1977.187.37, https://www.metmuseum.org/art/collection/search/310283.

46   "What Is Charye?," National Folk Museum of Korea, November 13, 2020, https://www.nfm.go.kr/english/subIndex/1046.do.

47   Na Sang-Hyeon and Sohn Dong-Joo, "Young Koreans Abandon Outdated Ancestral Rituals for Simple Gatherings," *Korea JoongAng Daily*, September 28, 2023, https://koreajoongangdaily.joins.com/news/2023-09-28/business/economy/Young-Koreans-abandon-outdated-ancestral-rituals-for-simple-gatherings/1875339.

48   Ebenstein, *Death*, 328.

49   Bryan Greene, "For Harry Houdini, Séances and Spiritualism Were Just an Illusion," *Smithsonian*, October 28, 2021, https://

www.smithsonianmag.com/history/for-harry-houdini
-seances-and-spiritualism-were-just-an-illusion-180978944/.

50 Grant Shreve, "When Women Channeled the Dead to Be
Heard," JSTOR Daily, February 2, 2018, https://daily.jstor.org
/when-women-channeled-the-dead-to-be-heard/.

51 Ebenstein, *Death*, p. 326. This section is by Elizabeth Harper,
a writer and lecturer on Catholic relics and oddities.

52 Stephen Garrigues, "Shamanism in Korea," Korean
Shamanism (website), February 15, 2016, https://shamanism
.sgarrigues.net/.

53 George Lawton, "Spiritualism—a Contemporary American
Religion," *Journal of Religion* 10, no. 1 (January 1930): 37–38,
http://www.jstor.org/stable/1196951.

54 Theresa Bane, *Encyclopedia of Spirits and Ghosts in World
Mythology* (McFarland, 2016).

55 Harriet Sherwood, "Church of England Could Seek
to End Paupers' Funerals," *Guardian*, January 26, 2020,
https://www.theguardian.com/society/2020/jan/26
/church-of-england-could-seek-end-paupers-funerals.

56 Thomas Laqueur, "Bodies, Death, and Pauper Funerals,"
Representations 1 (February 1983): 109, https://doi.org
/10.2307/3043762.

57 Doug Smith and Ruben Vives, "Homelessness Continues to
Soar, Jumping 9% in L.A. County, 10% in the City," *Los Angeles Times*, June 29, 2023, https://www.latimes.com/california
/story/2023-06-29/la-county-homelessness-unhoused
-population-count-jumps-increase.

58 Caitlin Doughty, *Smoke Gets in Your Eyes: And Other Lessons
from the Crematory* (W. W. Norton & Company, 2014), 202–3.

59 "Homeless Persons' Memorial Day," National Health Care
for the Homeless Council, August 2, 2019, https://nhchc.org
/consumers/events/homeless-persons-memorial-day/.

60 Waters, "Chinese Funerals," 104–34.

61 Doughty, *From Here to Eternity*, 165.

62 Colin Renfrew, "The Social Archaeology of Megalithic Monuments," *Scientific American* 249, no. 5 (November 1983): 152,
http://www.jstor.org/stable/24969036.

63 Kiki Karoglou, "Ancient and Modern Colossal Statues: From
Athena Parthenos to the Statue of Liberty," *Now at the Met*
(blog), July 1, 2016, https://www.metmuseum.org/blogs/now
-at-the-met/2016/ancient-and-modern-colossal-statues.

64 Rosemarie Trentinella, "Roman Portrait Sculpture: Republi-
can Through Constantinian," *Heilbrunn Timeline of Art History*
(blog), October 2003, https://www.metmuseum.org/toah/hd
/ropo/hd_ropo.htm.

65 Tim Edensor, "The Haunting Presence of Commemorative
Statues," *Ephemera: Theory & Politics in Organization* 19, no. 1
(2019): 56.

66 This quote was attributed to Lawrence A. Kuznar, then a
professor of anthropology at Indiana University–Purdue
University Fort Wayne. See "Historic Statue Removal—Top 3
Pros & Cons," ProCon.org, last updated on July 6, 2023,
https://www.procon.org/headlines/historic-statue-removal
-top-3-pros-cons/.

67 Philip Dwyer and Nikolas Orr, "Smashing Statues:
Re-evaluating Iconoclasm in History," *English Historical
Review* 138, no. 592 (June 2023): 429, https://doi.org/10.1093
/ehr/cead100.

68 Gary Younge, "Why Every Single Statue Should Come
Down," *Guardian*, June 1, 2021, https://www.theguardian.com
/artanddesign/2021/jun/01/gary-younge-why-every-single
-statue-should-come-down-rhodes-colston.

69 *Commemorative Naming in the United States* (US Geological
Survey, 1999), https://pubs.usgs.gov/fs/1999/0158/report.pdf.

70 Maoz Azaryahu, "The Power of Commemorative Street
Names," *Environment and Planning D: Society and Space* 14,
no. 3 (June 1996): 312, https://doi.org/10.1068/d140311.

71 Azaryahu, "The Power of Commemorative Street
Names," 319.

72 Azaryahu, 320.

73 Jim Kent, "South Dakota Leaders Object to Harney Peak
Name Change," *Lakota Times*, August 18, 2016, https://www
.lakotatimes.com/articles/south-dakota-leaders-object-to
-harney-peak-name-change/.

74 Myriam Houssay-Holzschuch and Frédéric Giraut, *The
Politics of Place Naming: Naming the World* (John Wiley &
Sons, 2022), 30–31.

75 Brandon Ecoffey, "Solemn Ceremony Marks Black Elk Peak
Renaming," *Lakota Times*, August 31, 2017, https://www
.lakotatimes.com/articles/solemn-ceremony-marks-black
-elk-peak-renaming/.

76 In places like Iceland, names are patronymic; this means
that a child takes the given name of their father (or occasionally their mother) as their last name, with a suffix of
either *-dóttir* for a daughter or *-son* for a son (duh). For
example, Olafur, the son of Haraldur Hreinsson, would
have "Haraldsson," not "Hreinsson," as a last name.

77 Greg Melville, *Over My Dead Body: Unearthing the Hidden
History of America's Cemeteries* (Abrams Press, 2022), 142.

78 "Tomb of the Unknown Soldier," US Department of Defense,
November 9, 2021, https://www.defense.gov/multimedia
/experience/tomb-of-the-unknown-soldier/.

79 "Tomb of the Unknown Soldier."

80 Dean and Chapter of Westminster, "Unknown Warrior,"
Westminster Abbey (website), June 12, 2018, https://www
.westminster-abbey.org/abbey-commemorations
/commemorations/unknown-warrior.

81 Centre des monuments nationaux, "The Unknown Soldier,"
Arc de Triomphe (website), July 11, 2023, https://www
.paris-arc-de-triomphe.fr/en/discover/the-unknown-soldier.

82 Vittoriano e Palazzo Venezia, "The Tomb of the Unknown
Soldier," VIVE, February 15, 2023, https://vive.cultura.gov.it
/en/altar-fatherland/not-miss/tomb-unknown-soldier.

83 John Pike, "Monument to the Unknown Soldier,"
GlobalSecurity.Org, accessed September 12, 2024, https://
www.globalsecurity.org/military/world/iraq/unknown
-soldier-dg.htm.

84 Johan Åhr, "Memory and Mourning in Berlin: On Peter Eisenman's *Holocaust-Mahnmal* (2005)," *Modern Judaism* 28, no. 3 (2008): 285, http://www.jstor.org/stable/30133319.

85 "Vietnam Veterans Memorial," US Department of Defense, April 1, 2022, https://www.defense.gov/Multimedia /Experience/Vietnam-Veterans-Memorial/.

86 Richard Brody, "The Inadequacy of Berlin's 'Memorial to the Murdered Jews of Europe,'" *New Yorker*, July 12, 2012, https://www.newyorker.com/culture/richard-brody/the -inadequacy-of-berlins-memorial-to-the-murdered-jews -of-europe.

87 Steve Inskeep, "Vietnam Veterans' Memorial Founder: Monument Almost Never Got Built," NPR, April 30, 2015, https://www.npr.org/2015/04/30/403034599/vietnam -veterans-memorial-founder-monument-almost -never-got-built.

Living: Notes on Dying

1 From *The Fire Next Time*. See "James Baldwin Among the Philosophers," UChicago Library, April 19, 2021, https://www .lib.uchicago.edu/collex/exhibits/james-baldwin-among -philosophers/.

2 James Gire, "How Death Imitates Life: Cultural Influences on Conceptions of Death and Dying," *Online Readings in Psychology and Culture* 6, no. 2 (December 2014): 6, https:// doi.org/10.9707/2307-0919.1120.

3 Gire, "How Death Imitates Life," 7.

4 Not just in the West—Chinese culture is notoriously defiant about death.

5 Andrew Bernstein, "Fire and Earth: The Forging of Modern Cremation in Meiji Japan," *Japanese Journal of Religious Studies* 27, no. 3/4 (Fall 2000): 301, http://www.jstor.org/stable /30233668.

6 Impermanence, "What Is Death Cafe?" Death Cafe, September 9, 2013, https://deathcafe.com/what/.

7 Daewoung Kim and Youngseo Choi, "Dying for a Better Life: South Koreans Fake Their Funerals for Life Lessons," Reuters, November 6, 2019, https://www.reuters.com/article /lifestyle/dying-for-a-better-life-south-koreans-fake-their -funerals-for-life-lessons-idUSKBN1XG037/.

8 The Order of the Good Death, "Our Work," May 22, 2022, https://www.orderofthegooddeath.com/our-work.

9 Margareta Magnusson, *The Gentle Art of Swedish Death Cleaning: How to Free Yourself and Your Family from a Lifetime of Clutter* (Simon & Schuster, 2018).

10 Caitlin Doughty, *Smoke Gets in Your Eyes: And Other Lessons from the Crematory* (W. W. Norton & Company, 2014), 43.

11 Doughty, *Smoke Gets in Your Eyes*, 43.

12 Jennifer M. Strickland, *Palliative Pharmacy Care* (ASHP, 2014), 7.

13 Strickland, *Palliative Pharmacy Care*, 8–9.

14 Judith Garber, "The Medicalization of Death: What Does It Mean and What Can We Do About It?," Lown Institute, February 7, 2022, https://lowninstitute.org/how-death-became -medicalized-and-what-we-can-do-about-it/.

15 Sheri Fink, "Atul Gawande's 'Being Mortal,'" *The New York Times*, November 6, 2014, https://www.nytimes.com /2014/11/09/books/review/atul-gawande-being-mortal -review.html.

16 Abby Ellin, "'Death Doulas' Provide Aid at the End of Life," *The New York Times*, June 24, 2021, https://www.nytimes.com /2021/06/24/well/doulas-death-end-of-life.html.

17 Prisoners on death row in Japan are notified of their executions on the day they are put to death. See "Death-Row Prisoners in Japan Sue Over Same-Day Notice of Executions," Death Penalty Information Center, updated June 11, 2024, https://deathpenaltyinfo.org/news/death-row -prisoners-in-japan-sue-over-same-day-notice-of -executions.

18 *Amnesty International Global Report: Death Sentences and Executions 2022* (Amnesty International, 2023), https://www .amnesty.org/en/documents/act50/6548/2023/en/.

19 "Death Row Overview," Death Penalty Information Center, accessed September 13, 2024, https://deathpenaltyinfo.org /death-row/overview.

20 "Time on Death Row," Death Penalty Information Center, September 18, 2019, https://deathpenaltyinfo.org/death-row /death-row-time-on-death-row.

21 Heather L. Weaver, "The Final Religious Request of a Man on Death Row Is in the Supreme Court's Hands," American Civil Liberties Union, November 8, 2021, https://www.aclu .org/news/prisoners-rights/the-final-religious-request-of-a -man-on-death-row-is-in-the-supreme-courts-hands.

22 Juan A. Lozano and Michael Graczyk, "Texas Executes
    Inmate Who Fought Prayer, Touch Rules," *AP News*,
    October 5, 2022, https://apnews.com/article/us
    -supreme-court-texas-prisons-religion-prayer
    -9d424be517314cbf2b59543a22d47fa4.

23 Sarah L. Gerwig-Moore, Andrew Davies, and Sabrina Atkins,
    "Cold (Comfort?) Food: The Significance of Last Meal Rituals
    in the United States," *British Journal of American Legal Studies*
    3, no. 2 (Fall 2014): 421, https://digitalcommons.law.mercer
    .edu/cgi/viewcontent.cgi?article=1003&context=fac_pubs.

24 Gerwig-Moore, Davies, and Atkins, "Cold (Comfort?)
    Food," 417.

25 Gerwig-Moore, Davies, and Atkins, 418.

26 Gerwig-Moore, Davies, and Atkins, 411.

27 Mary Roach, *Stiff: The Curious Lives of Human Cadavers*
    (W. W. Norton & Company, 2003), 43–44.

28 Hayley Campbell, *All the Living and the Dead: A Personal Inves-
    tigation into the Death Trade* (Raven Books, 2022), 30–31.

29 Campbell, *All the Living and the Dead*, 31.

30 Referring to the Burke and Hare murders.

31 "Organ Donation Statistics," Health Resources & Services
    Administration, July 5, 2021, https://www.organdonor.gov
    /learn/organ-donation-statistics.

32 Caitlin Doughty, *From Here to Eternity: Traveling the World to
    Find the Good Death* (W. W. Norton & Company, 2017), 111.

33 Hannah Ritchie and Edouard Mathieu, "How Many People
    Die and How Many Are Born Each Year?," Our World in
    Data, January 5, 2023, https://ourworldindata.org/births
    -and-deaths.

34 *Oxford English Dictionary*, "humane," accessed Decem-
    ber 2023, https://doi.org/10.1093/OED/2650323806.

35 Beth A. Conklin, *Consuming Grief: Compassionate Cannibalism
    in an Amazonian Society* (University of Texas Press, 2001), xx.

36 Frank Shyong, "Lunar New Year Traditions Were Abstract
    Until My Grandmother Died," *Los Angeles Times*, February 21,
    2024, https://www.latimes.com/california/story/2024-02-21
    /lunar-tradition-grandma.

Acknowledgments

This book would not exist without my army of editors, both official and unofficial. Thank you to Natalie Butterfield, Isabel Hinchliff, Brittany McInerney, and all the good folks over at Chronicle, who believed in me and gently guided me through the bookmaking process, step by arduous step. Special shoutout to my designers, Wynne and Barbara, who had to contend with the most last-minute illustrator of all time and remained a joy to collaborate with through it all.

The fattest, warmest thank you to my friends Cherie, Yoonjung, Yoonjoo, Laurain, and Monika, who were my first readers, assistant researchers, critics, and fact-checkers. Thank you to all my friends in New York and Singapore who kept me nourished, motivated, and at least semi-socialized throughout my long stint in book-writing hermitage—I could not have done this without you.

Thank you to my professors over at MICA, especially Lisa Perrin and Shadra Strickland, who not only shaped the way I see the world and my craft but were also pivotal in helping me chisel this book out of a block of rough marble during my senior year of college.

Thank you to all the historians, researchers, anthropologists, and writers who laid the groundwork for this project. It is an interesting world we live in, and there is so much more to learn.

The biggest thank you of all to my parents, from whom I inherited all my curiosity and wit. I wrote this book because of (and maybe for) my dad, who in his old age has grown increasingly aware of his own mortality, and in our talks made me more aware of mine. I started writing this book during the pandemic, and I think I saw it as an escape. What I've found at the end is that there is no escape—not from death, not from fear, and not from grief. But what I've also learned from the myriad of death rituals I've had the pleasure to research is that there is no need to run from it. Death is death, like trees are trees and water is water. Pain will come, because the love was there. And it is a blessing to be surrounded by people you are afraid to lose.

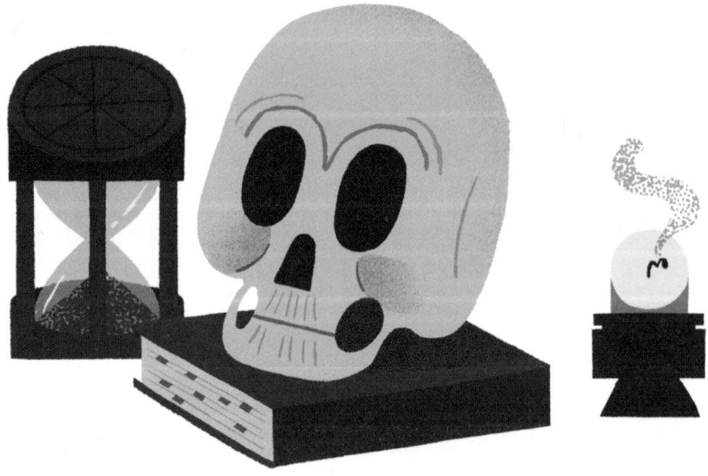